W9-CJN-827

UNIVERSITY OF WINNIPEG
515 PORTAGE AVE.
WINNIPEG, MAN.

DISCARDED

THE OLD ENGLISH
CHRISTIAN EPIC

NOTE.

All references to lines of the poems are for the *Juliana* to Strunk's edition, for the *Elene* to Kent's, for the *Andreas* to Krapp's, for the *Christ* to Cook's and for the *Beowulf* to Wyatt's. For these I have occasionally used the abbreviations Strunk, Kent, Krapp, Cook, and Wyatt.

PR
1667
.P6 S6
1971

THE OLD ENGLISH CHRISTIAN EPIC

A STUDY IN THE PLOT TECHNIQUE OF
THE JULIANA, THE ELENE, THE ANDREAS,
AND THE CHRIST,
IN COMPARISON WITH THE BEOWULF
AND WITH THE LATIN LITERATURE
OF THE MIDDLE AGES

By

GEORGE ARNOLD SMITHSON

Phaeton Press

New York

1971

Originally Published 1910

Reprinted 1971

Published by PHAETON PRESS, INC.

Library of Congress Catalog Card Number - 75-128192

SBN 87753-050-5

CONTENTS

A STUDY IN THE PLOT TECHNIQUE OF
THE JULIANA, THE ELENE, THE ANDREAS,
AND THE CHRIST,
IN COMPARISON WITH THE BEOWULF
AND WITH THE LATIN LITERATURE
OF THE MIDDLE AGES

I.

THE GENERAL RELATION OF THE OLD ENGLISH CHRISTIAN POEMS TO LATIN LITERATURE.

When we glance over the body of Old English poetry, we notice that the longer works fall into two main groups. In the one stands alone the *Beowulf*; in the other stand the Cædmonian and Cynewulfian poems which I shall term "the Christian epics."[1] The *Beowulf* has been examined adequately both as to matter and as to form. The Christian epics have been examined adequately as to matter but not as to form. The former belongs in effect largely to the period which preceded Christianity. The latter are products of Christian England. Hence we may expect the Christian epics to differ in form from the *Beowulf*, to be strongly affected in form by the influences which came in the train of Christianity, as they have been shown to be strongly influenced in matter.[2]

This expectation becomes *a priori* almost certainty when we consider for a moment what the introduction of Christianity meant to early England. When St. Augustine established Christianity in Kent in 597, Canterbury became an important center of Latin learning. In 635, Aidan, an Irish monk from Iona, entered Northumbria and spread Christianity southward. There was founded the monastery of Whitby, the scene of the tradition of Cædmon. The year 668 saw the arrival of three noted students and teachers, Theodore of Tarsus, who had studied Greek at Athens, Benedict Biscop or Baducing, a Northumbrian noble who had returned from his second visit to Rome and founded the schools of St. Peter and St. Paul near Jarrow on the Tyne, and Adrian or Hadrian, an African monk who went to the school at Canterbury. The monastic schools founded by

---

[1] There is little or no evidence for the theory that the Beowulf is not an independent product of the English or the Teutonic genius, that the larger kind of heroic poem was attained in England only through the example of Latin narrative. The present work is strong evidence to the contrary.

[2] See Strunk, Kent, Krapp, and Cook.

such men created a new life of the intellect. Biscop's pupil at
Jarrow, the Venerable Bede, was one of six hundred students.
The school at York which produced Alcuin became the center
of learning in Europe. To it flocked students from Ireland,
Gaul, Germany, and Italy.[3]

The students at these schools read the classic Latin of Vergil,
the Latin of those who imitated Vergil in matter and form, the
Latin of the Christian poems which imitated the form of the
Vergilian, the Latin of classic and medieval prose, the Latin
legends of saints, and the Latin works of the fathers. The library
at York contained the works of Vergil, Statius, Lucan, Auctor,
Sedulius, Juvencus, Clemens, Prosper, Paulinus, Arator, Pom-
peius, Pliny, Cicero, Probus, Focas, Donatus, Priscian, Servitus,
Euticius, Comminianus, Lactantius, Aldhelm, Bede, Victorinus,
Boethius, Jerome, Hilary, Ambrose, Augustine, Athanasius,
Orosius, Gregory the Great, Pope Leo, Basil, Fulgentius, Cas-
siodorus, Chrysostom, and John.[4] Aldhelm in a letter to Acircius
quotes from Vergil, Ovid, Lucan, Cicero, Pliny, Sallust, Solinus,
Juvencus, Sedulius, Arator, Alcimus Avitus, Prudentius, Prosper,
Corippus, Venantius Fortunatus, Paulinus of Périgueux, and
Paulus Quaestor.[5] And when we examine the Latin prose of
Bede's *Ecclesiastical History* and the Latin verse of Alcuin's
De Pontificibus, we become convinced that men like Cædmon
and Cynewulf must have been influenced profoundly by Latin
literature.

In view of this, it was my purpose in undertaking a study of
the Old English Christian epic to restrict myself to the influence
of the Latin upon the form of the Cynewulfian poems. But
when I came to look for evidence to prove my conviction that
the form of the Cynewulfian poems was profoundly influenced
by that of the Latin, I was forced to admit that that conviction,
although it is a natural one, is in most respects a mistaken one.
It is true that the Latin works which were read in English
schools were of the greatest importance in inciting Englishmen

---

3 Pancoast, *Introduction to English Literature*, pp. 30-33. Green, *A History of the English People*, book I, chap. II.

4 Alcuin, *De Pontificibus*, ll. 1534-1561.

5 *Cambridge History of English Literature*, vol. I, p. 84.

to literary effort. In a time when most of the older poetry was looked upon as hostile to the Christian religion, or at least as doing nothing for the advancement of Christianity, it is possible that there would have been no important efforts toward literary expression, if there had been no examples of Latin religious poetry in the libraries of the monastic schools. The *Beowulf* might have been lost to Christian England had it not been for the tendency manifested in the Latin works of interpreting pagan products as Christian allegories or of adding to them lines which showed the Christian lesson to be drawn from the pagan story.[6] Again, the fact that the Old English poems were written down at all shows the influence of Latin culture, especially when we consider that those poems were written in the letters of the Latin alphabet.[7]

Then it is true that the subject matter of the *Elene,* the *Juliana,* the *Christ,* and probably the *Andreas* was supplied by the Latin, as has been shown conclusively.[8] But, when we were led *a priori* to the conclusion that the form of the Old English religious poems as well as the matter was profoundly influenced by the Latin, we did not have in mind the nature of the Christian's regard for the works of Vergil and his pagan followers and the nature of the Latin Christian poems.

Ecclesiastical writers were strongly opposed to pagan works of literature. The authors of lives of saints naturally held that it was better to read their works than to study the doings of the pagan Aeneas. Juvencus expounds this view in the preface to his versification of the Gospels; and Bede writes:

> Bella Maro resonet, nos pacis dona canamus,
> Munera nos Christi, bella Maro resonet.[9]

Augustine, who earlier had found much pleasure in Vergil, looks with regret upon the days when he wept over the death of Dido, ''quia se occidit ob amorem, cum interea me ipsum in his a te morientem, deus vita mea, siccis oculis ferrem miserri-

---

[6] See the interpretation of the myth of Orpheus and Eurydice in the Alfredian version of *De Consolatione Philosophiae* of Boethius, XXXV, ed. Sedgefield, p. 103, and the allegories of the Phoenix, the Panther, the Whale, the Partridge.

[7] Comparetti, *Virgil in the Middle Ages,* pp. 240-241.

[8] See Strunk, Kent, Krapp, and Cook.

[9] *Historia Ecclesiastica,* ed. Stevenson, p. 295.

mus.'"[10] "Alcuin, who had in his youth, as his anonymous biographer puts it, read 'the books of the philosophers and the lies of Vergil' and at the age of eleven preferred Vergil to the Psalms,[11] when he became old, refused to have anything more to do with such things, and forbade his disciples to read the *Aeneid*, saying, 'The divine poets are enough, nor is there any need that you should be contaminated by the sensuous eloquence of Vergil.' "[12] In the preface to his commentary on the Song of Solomon Alcuin writes:

> Haec rogo menti iuvenis mandare memento,
> carmina sunt nimium falsi haec meliora Maronis
> haec tibi vera canunt vitae praecepta perennis,
> auribus ille tuis male frivola falsa sonabit.[13]

And Jerome recounts the dream in which the Judge of Man exclaims, "Thou a Christian! Thou art a Ciceronian! Where the heart is, there is its treasure."[14]

But the pagan Latin works continued to be studied in spite of all opposition. Latin was the language of the church. And in order to be able to read, write and speak Latin it was necessary to study it. However, the study of Latin in the schools was primarily only the study of grammar. The supreme authority for grammar was Vergil. The study of Vergil meant in general nothing but the study of grammar.[15] "Virgil—was no longer Virgil, but incarnate grammar and authoritative history."[16] Since the works of Vergil were read, they were necessarily of some influence upon the writings of the Christians. This is evident from the recurrence of quotations from Vergil in the works of those who most vigorously opposed profane studies. Augustine made use of Vergil in his *De Civitate Dei;* and there is a manuscript of Vergil in the library of Berne supposed to have been written by Alcuin.[17] This influence, however, was not

---

[10] *S. Aureli Augustini confessionum*, lib. I, c. 13.

[11] *Vit. Beati Alcuini*, Act. S. iv, 147.

[12] Comparetti, *Vergil in the Middle Ages*, p. 91.

[13] *Monumenta Alcuiniana*, ed. Hattenbach and Duemmler, p. 714, quoted by Comparetti, *Vergil in the Middle Ages*, pp. 88-91.

[14] Epist. xxii ad Eustochium. Taylor, *The Classical Heritage of the Middle Ages*, p. 109.

[15] Comparetti, *Vergil in the Middle Ages*, pp. 75-77.

[16] Taylor, *The Classical Heritage of the Middle Ages*, p. 3.

[17] Müller, *Analecta Bernensia*, iii, pp. 23-25. Comparetti, p. 91.

of the vital kind that results from the full appreciation of a
work of art with its content and its form inseparable. It was
largely the influence of grammar and diction upon the Latin of
the churchmen. It was the influence of form upon subject-
matter which was in itself foreign to that form.

With the supremacy of Christianity, Latin poetry of classical
form, 'being an artificial product, is in the hands of the clergy
and occupies itself mainly with religion; with sentiments or
emotions of any other character it is not concerned, for even
when its subject is secular, as for instance in the versified
accounts of historical events, the nature of the ideas and the
moral reflections shows clearly that the point of view is always
strictly clerical and religious—It was not the expression of an
emotion or a sentiment, it was not even the intelligent imitation
of a definite type of art.'[18]

When Prudentius, the most read of the Christian poets, and
Juvencus, who put into hexameters the life of Christ, imitated
Vergil, they produced works 'in which the convictions, the argu-
ments, the moralizings might be sincere enough, but in which the
real poetry of Christianity could have but little part.'[19]

Cynewulf might have written this sort of poetry, if he had
imitated the form of the *Aeneid* or of the Latin religious poems
which copied it. He did not do so. He chose, instinctively,
probably, the form of the Old English heroic epic which had
been developed in accord with the spirit of his people. When
he adopted this form, better adapted to the expression of his
thoughts and feelings, he showed the same wisdom as did Chaucer,
when he chose English as the medium for his expression, and
Dante, when he chose Italian. For this we should be grateful to
Cynewulf, since had his art been more imitative of the Latin
products, his poetry would have been more artificial, less strong
as a national, natural work of literature.

Christian Latin poetry did not always remain an artificial
imitation of classical forms. Christian feeling was too real to lie
long without a natural mode of expression. ''Breaking down the
barrier of classical forms which imprisoned it, it found a vehicle

---

[18] Comparetti, pp. 161-162

[19] Comparetti, p. 160.

of expression in that simple and vulgar Latin which had grown up under the influence of the time and remained the regular organ of the Christian liturgy and faith. Disregarding the quantity and following only the stress, it associated itself with that popular poetry which was the natural outcome of the new rhythms resulting from the intonation peculiar to the new spoken languages."[20]

This new Latin poetry was a natural form of expression for the spirit of the time. It was a form which would serve more naturally for the expression of the Old English Christian spirit in the Old English language. And Cynewulf, who did not allow the artificial imitations of Vergil to determine the form of such poems as the *Juliana* and the *Elene,* showed himself open to the influence of the new Latin literature in the form of the *Christ* which stands apart from the more purely narrative products of the Old English genius, a new type, but a natural, effective one.

Then, too, the Christian Latin prose, particularly that of the Church service, which was developed in accord with the spirit of the time, was, as we shall point out, of influence upon the Old English poems.

Now, since the influence of the Latin epics upon the form of the Old English Christian poems was not so vital as one might at first be led to suppose, we are justified in regarding the question of the relation between the two as a minor one in our study of Cynewulf. And since Cynewulf was not a mere literal translator, since he did not reproduce foreign works as such in Old English, we shall be justified in studying his works as original products, in judging them intrinsically, without regard to their sources.

---

[20] Comparetti, *Vergil in the Middle Ages,* p. 164.

II.

FUNDAMENTAL CONCEPTION AND CENTRAL MOTIF.

The fundamental conception of the *Juliana,* the *Elene,* and the *Andreas* is Christianity *versus* paganism or Judaism. In each case it is the combination of a single, dominant thought, a single controlling passion, and a single mood of the mind. It involves the two essential interests of the Old English life of its time, violent action, with the pagan ideals of strength, loyalty, courage, revenge, generosity, wisdom, and acquiescence in the decrees of fate, and Christianity, with the new ideals of love, faith, and self-sacrifice.

This fundamental conception is developed by the conflicting interests of the new religion and the old. On the one side is Juliana, Elene, or Andrew assisted by God and the angels; on the other are the pagans or the Jews aided by the devil. In the end God's power manifested through his followers triumphs over the forces of the devil and brings about a final victory for Christianity.

In the *Christ* the fundamental conception is the coming of the Lord. It is a combination of a single mood of the mind, the spirit of Advent, and a single dominant thought, the lesson to be drawn from the Advent. It portrays the mind of the individual in praise of God for the coming of the Savior in the flesh, in thanksgiving to God for the coming of the Holy Spirit to the soul of the believer, and in awe of God for the final coming to judge mankind. This portrayal of the spirit of Advent is combined with the dominant thought that it is right and expedient to serve the true God, wrong and inexpedient to serve the devil. Again there are involved the two essential interests of Old English life, violent action and Christianity, although the first has less place than in the other poems. Here the fundamental conception is developed by a series of representations of the emotions of the believer expressed in hymns, prayers, and thanksgivings, by a series of pictures of Christ's Ascension and of the

Day of Doom, and by a series of lessons drawn from those pictures.

The fundamental conception in each of these poems is high and universally human. Each deals with the outer and inner life of men who do and dare and who have sufficient spiritual grounds for their action; with the relation of the transitory, earthly life to the eternal life which is to follow; with the requital of the deeds of the flesh by rewards or punishments after death. Each deals with the powers of man as a physical being and as a spiritual being trusting in and aided by a force greater than himself. The fact that this force, this superhuman element in the poems, plays a large part may make the fundamental conceptions appear weak to modern readers. In reality they are not weaker than the fundamental conception of the *Iliad*, the *Æneid*, or of any story which deals with superhuman powers or motifs. The superhuman element necessitates in modern readers a certain adjustment to the hypothesis upon which the story is based, that there is a superhuman power which may affect human affairs. But we must remember that the Englishmen for whom these stories were written did not require the mental adjustment that is required of us. The intervention of the superhuman in human affairs was for them one of the facts of life.

Then, in each of these poems the development of the fundamental conception shows the typical Christian treatment of a tragic theme. In the *Juliana*, while the theme of the story, the maid's fatal opposition to the laws of society as represented by the control of father over daughter, by the power of the ruler over the ruled, and by the force of national religion, is essentially tragic, the outcome partakes rather of the nature of serious comedy. The maiden meets death, it is true, but death means the glorious reward of Heaven. The *Elene* maintains a less tragic mood throughout the story. When the plot becomes tragic, as in case of the torture of Judas, it is only for the sake of making more effective the final purification of that character. The *Andreas*, like the *Juliana*, is essentially tragic in theme. The individual opposition of Andrew to the national idea of the Mermedonians should result naturally in the death of the hero. But the tragedy is averted at the end by the intervention of a superhuman power. Even those who have already met death are restored to life.· And in the *Christ,* finally, although the emphasis at the end is upon the destruction of the sinful, throughout the poem the hope of Heaven is held before the eyes of the reader, and at the end the joys of eternal life with God are awarded to those who have kept His commandments.

CENTRAL MOTIF.

In dealing with the fundamental conceptions of these poems it is important to note that, while in each case we have a blending of the ideals of the old religion with those of the new, we have in no instance a central motif that is not Christian.

In the *Juliana* the heroine exhibits the greatest valor in her sufferings and in overcoming the devil. Yet never is valor in itself the central motif. She acts as she does in order to gain the life of joy with Christ. The destruction of the pagans by molten lead and by drowning exhibits the old ideal of revenge. Yet never is revenge an end in itself. It is the just punishment of a supreme God. Revenge in itself as a motif is shown only in the father of Juliana and in Heliseus, the villains of the story, where it serves to emphasize by contrast the absence of the spirit of revenge in the heroine.

Again, Elene like a crusader sets out with her armed band. Her action in starving Judas in revenge for his refusal to disclose the cross seems to be anything but Christian in spirit; but valor or revenge is never the mainspring of action. Elene's treatment of Judas has for its motif her Christian zeal. Personal revenge has no place in the story.

So, too, in the *Andreas* the apostles go to the land of the cannibal Mermedonians as vikings on their raids. Andrew seems to aim not only at spiritual triumph but also at temporal. He causes the destruction of the guards and calls forth the flood as the old pagan hero would do in revenge for his tortures. Yet revenge in itself does not move him. He punishes the pagans in order to win them to Christ. Here the devil and the Mermedonians manifest the spirit of personal revenge as an end in itself, but here, as in the *Juliana,* this spirit serves to emphasize by contrast the Christianity of the hero.

Finally in the *Christ* the central motif of praise to God for His coming to man combined with zeal to save souls is again essentially Christian. This poem, too, shows the older pagan ideals. One of the joys of the blessed is the view of the tortures of the damned. And the doom of the wicked' at the last great day is Christ's revenge upon mankind. But the damned meet their fates, not through the personal hatred of their foes, but through the just decisions of the Judge who sorrows in their punishment.

COMPARISON WITH THE BEOWULF AND WITH THE LATIN.

Thus the Cynewulfian poems, in which valor for its own sake never becomes the mainspring of action, and in which hatred and revenge only emphasize by contrast Christian love and forgiveness, stand in marked contrast to the *Beowulf*. In the last the fundamental conception, how a hero conquered monsters in revenge for their injuries to the folk, does not introduce the ideas or the ideals of Christianity. The pagan ideals of strength, loyalty, courage, revenge, generosity, wisdom, and acquiescence in the decrees of fate are manifested in the development of the fundamental conception. The Christian ideals of love, faith, and self-sacrifice are absolutely wanting. The central motif by which the fundamental conception is developed in the *Beowulf* is the hero's valor. There are many subsidiary motifs which emphasize this central one by comparison and by contrast. But there is nowhere a specifically Christian motif. Zeal for Christ is not the motif for a single one of Beowulf's actions. Nor is the opposition of the monsters in any case due to zeal for the devil. It is true that Grendel is said to be of the race of Cain (107-114; 1258-1268), but it is also true that Grendel's opposition is said positively to be due to the noise in the Hall (86-89). The opposition of Grendel's mother is due to her desire to avenge the death of her son (1276-1278). And the opposition of the dragon is due to inherent hatred for mankind, to love of treasure, and to revenge for the plundering of the hoard (2278-2311). It is nowhere noted that Hrothgar's relief from Grendel results in his conversion to Christianity. The poem mentions the fact that Hrothgar knew not the true God (178-183) before the arrival of

Beowulf, although he discourses later as a confirmed Christian (1700-1784).

This distinct difference between the *Beowulf* on the one hand and the Cynewulfian poems on the other, the fact that the Beowulf with its abundance of Christian moralizings has nothing of Christianity in its fundamental conception and motivation, seems to me to be very positive evidence that the *Beowulf* is not more than a weakly Christianized pagan poem. It puts aside, to my mind, once for all, the theory that Cynewulf is the author of the Beowulf.

It is not necessary for us to take up the relation between the fundamental conceptions and central motifs of the Cynewulfian poems and those of the Latin, since this question has been treated adequately in studies of the sources of the *Juliana,* the *Elene,* the *Andreas,* and the *Christ*

III.

GENERAL FORM.

THE JULIANA, THE ELENE, AND THE ANDREAS.

The general form which is employed to develop the fundamental conceptions of the *Juliana*, the *Elene*, and the *Andreas* is
the narrative poem. The author wrote a story in each case,
because, although his main purpose was probably to turn folk to
Christ, he was too artistic to be wholly didactic. He had been
stirred undoubtedly by the old heroic tales of his race; he had
seen the folk spell-bound by the recital of the minstrel; he had
realized that the people could not be drawn from the vivid, pagan
narrative by the didactic, Christian sermon. Consequently he
wrote a story which would serve to take the place of the older
narratives and at the same time promote the cause of the true
God. On account of the influence of the older tales, too, he
wrote poetry rather than prose. The old heroic, alliterative
measures were a form familiar to him and to his audience, a
form which had become traditional with the Old English people,
a form far more forcible than prose in an age when stories were
heard, not read. Moreover, the author was by nature poetic. He
was capable of expressing his thought and his emotion in the
form of poetry and his spirit moved him to do so.

These narrative poems are what I have termed Christian epics.
By this I mean simply that they are narrative poems in the
Old English language, of religious legends, written in an
approximation to the manner of the 'natural' or Homeric epic
by a self-conscious individual whose own religious emotions pre-
vented his work from being purely objective.

THE CHRIST.

We are justified in including the *Christ* under the term
'Christian epic' only by the fact that the word epic has been
applied to almost every sort of long poem in elevated style. The
Christ is lacking to a great extent in the element of narrative

objectivity which is regarded, probably, as the most essential quality of the epic. Narrative is wanting in Part I, and has only a small place in Part II, although it becomes stronger in the pictures of the events of the Day of Doom in Part III. The poem is for the greater part lyric and expository, not narrative. Yet we must remember that the *Christ* has many epic characteristics.

COMPARISON WITH THE BEOWULF AND WITH THE LATIN.

The general form of the *Juliana,* the *Elene,* and the *Andreas* is essentially that of the Old English pagan epic. The Latin epics of Vergil and of Vergil's imitators, both pagan and Christian, were before the Old English poet. But how weak their influence was in comparison with that of the national, heroic epic is seen in the fact that we can recognize each characteristic of the general form of the Cynewulfian poem in the national, heroic epic. The *Juliana,* the *Elene,* and the *Andreas* are essentially in the language of the *Beowulf.* They are in the metrical form of the *Beowulf·* They are, like the *Beowulf,* narrative, while the Latin poems are more largely lyric and expository. And the structure and the style of the narrative in them are, as we shall see later, similar to the structure and the style of the narrative in the *Beowulf.*

The *Juliana,* the *Elene,* and the *Andreas* are, like the *Beowulf,* epics of the individual. In the *Juliana* our interest is aroused not at all in the outcome of a conflict between great masses of men as it is in the *Iliad.* The poem is the story of an individual even more than is the *Beowulf;* for in the latter, although our interest centers in the issues of Beowulf's fights with Grendel, with Grendel's mother, and with the fire dragon, yet we are concerned to a certain extent with the effects of Beowulf's deeds upon Hrothgar and his followers and upon Beowulf's own people. The *Elene* and the *Andreas,* too, are epics of the individual. However, our interest is not so exclusively in the main characters. We are concerned with the conflicts between the masses in the strife between Romans and barbarians, Christians and Jews, and Christians and pagans.

The *Christ,* also, deals largely with the individual, God or Christ. But here, more than in any of the other poems, we have the action which concerns great masses of men. God is the single individual dominating all; yet we are interested not so much in the acts of God as in the effects of those acts upon the hosts of those who are to be judged.

The general form of the *Christ,* as we shall see later, owes to the Latin much more than does the general form of the other poems. And we shall see also that, notwithstanding, there is much in the *Christ* that is closely related to the *Beowulf.*

IV.

UNITY, EMPHASIS, AND COHERENCE OF PLOT.

When we turn from the general form of the *Juliana*, of the *Elene*, of the *Andreas*, and of the *Christ* to a somewhat detailed examination of their plots, we find that each of the first three embraces one main event which is a unified, organic whole. In the *Juliana*, the conflict between the heroine and Heliseus, beginning with the maid's refusal to marry a pagan, is developed through the tortures inflicted upon her in the attempt to change her course of action to a definite end in the death of both hero and heroine. In the *Elene* the sending of the heroine to recover the cross is followed by her actions toward that end and the final accomplishment of her purpose. And in the *Andreas* the great conflict between Andrew and the cannibal Mermedonians is developed to its end in the conversion of the heathen.

But when we test these poems more strictly according to the principle of unity which demands that each part must contribute to the main effect, that no part may be omitted without detracting from that main effect, we find striking faults.

The introduction of the *Juliana* informs us of the time and the place of action, portrays briefly the main characters, Heliseus and Juliana, suggests the mood of the whole in the deadly conflict between Christianity and the older religion, and sets before us the situation,—the Christian maid betrothed to the heathen prince—from which the main action springs.

Then follows the point of first interest, from which we are held in suspense as to the outcome of Juliana's refusal to marry Heliseus through the successive punishments inflicted upon the maid, up to the point where the devil comes to her in the prison. This coming of the devil is an important part of the story. It is the supreme test of Juliana's faith, the temptation of the fiend himself. And the voice from the clouds, which answers Juliana's appeal to God, is also of importance, for with it comes the assurance of divine aid, the manifestation of divine power in Juliana when she binds the devil.

But the succeeding recital of the many crimes of the devil, expository in manner, is a tedious, didactic digression, which tends to dispel our interest in the main thread of action, the conflict between Juliana and Heliseus. It is true that this dry recital does serve to emphasize the fact that God has shown himself to be on the side of Juliana; but such emphasis contributes nothing to the story as a whole because the relation between Juliana and God is quite clear without it. The whole recital may be omitted without detraction from the effect of the story as it stands. It is worse than useless, since its tendency is to make us lose all interest in the outcome of the main action of the plot. Now, when we realize that in a poem of 731 lines, 242 lines[1] are given up to an expository digression which tends to destroy our interest in the outcome of the story, we must decide that the author shows a lamentable lack of the sense of perspective, or an equally lamentable substitution of a didactic purpose for an artistic one.

After this long digression, the story proceeds again along the main line of action, the conflict between Heliseus and Juliana, to their deaths at the end. The exhortation of Juliana to the heathen people (635-669), as she is led to her death, is again somewhat digressive and didactic, but it is in accord with the spirit of the whole and it strikes us as the natural expression of the Christian heroine as she goes to her death.

The introduction of the *Elene* (1-194) includes a brief description of the character of the Emperor Constantine, the account of the approach of the overwhelming hosts of the barbarians and of the preparations of the Romans to meet them, the description of Constantine's dream, and the account of the Roman victory which is followed by the interpretation of the dream and the baptism of the Emperor. Thus the introduction informs us of the time of the action and of the place of its beginning. It portrays the character not of the heroine of the story, but of the heroine's son, who has no place in the main action of the story proper. It suggests the mood of the whole in the victory of Christianity against enormous odds. And it informs us of the

---

[1] Probably from 65 to 75 lines of the digression are lost after l. 288, where a page of the manuscript is lost.

circumstances which brought the mind of the Emperor to the mood which prompted the journey for the recovery of the cross. This introduction, then, does contribute, although rather indirectly, to the outcome of the whole. It has not, however, the nature of a necessary part of that whole. The expedition in search of the cross would be an organic unit without it. The account of the dream of Constantine and the battle which follows it bears a very loose relation to the expedition of Elene. A stronger introduction would be that which would describe not Constantine but Elene, which would make the dream and the battle subordinate by interesting us in their outcome, not for itself or for its effect upon Constantine, but for its effect upon Elene.

Our interest in the main outcome is not aroused until after this introduction, when the Emperor, desirous of recovering the true cross, bids his mother fare to the land of the Jews to obtain it. From this point to the miracle which discloses the true cross (220-894) there is nothing which does not contribute towards the outcome. We have first the voyage to Jerusalem, then, the three councils of the Jews, the report of Judas, and the fourth council in which Judas is put forward as the spokesman. Next, Judas refuses to tell the secret and is thrust into a dried-up well. Finally he tells all and is led to Calvary, where God discloses the three crosses. Lastly, the cross of Christ is distinguished by the miracle of the dead man restored to life.

And no part of this may be omitted without detraction from the effect of the whole. It is true that at first thought it may occur to us that the story would not be harmed if the first three councils were reduced to two or even to one. It does seem that the three councils serve primarily to make room for the three religious discourses of Elene. But each of the three councils is necessary in order to strengthen our interest in the outcome, to maintain the suspense. Here we do not tend to lose interest in the main outcome, as we do in the *Juliana*. And the speeches of Elene and Judas, while they undoubtedly partake somewhat of the nature of sermons, are integral parts of the plot. Elene's speeches are necessary for bringing home the sin of the Jews to Judas, and Judas' are necessary as the causes of his becoming spokesman for the others.

The story should come to a close with the discovery of the true cross or with a brief conclusion informing us of the fate of Judas and of the disposal of the relic. Instead of this we have the unnecessary words of Judas and the devil (895-967), the account of the embassy to Constantine (968-1015), the building of the temple (1015-1033), and the baptism of Judas and his ordination as bishop (1033-1063). This long conclusion violates the principle of unity, as does the long introduction, for, while it is closely related to the rest of the story, it is not a necessary, organic part of that story.

The secondary plot of the *Elene,* which has to do with the finding of the nails, is closely connected with the main plot. The discovery of the cross leads Elene to desire to find the nails, and through the prayer of Judas again God discloses them. Then follows the conclusion which tells of the disposal of the nails. Now this secondary plot, as it stands, violates the principle of unity, as it is not a necessary part of the story. This is not to say that the material of the secondary plot might not have been embodied in the whole without destroying its unity. The finding of the nails is not a new story connected with the first merely by the fact that the same character is concerned in each, as is the case with the second part of the *Beowulf.* The fault here is that the secondary plot seems to be an unnecessary addition tacked on at the end. The fault lies in the violation of the principles of emphasis and coherence more than in the violation of the principle of unity.

After the secondary plot follows the natural conclusion of the whole, the success of the new bishop and the departure of Elene.

Finally, before leaving the subject of unity, we should mention that the *Elene* is greatly weakened by the fact that there are three main protagonists. The introduction leads us to suppose that the plot is to be concerned primarily with the actions of Constantine. But Constantine practically drops out of the story, and we follow Elene as the heroine. Then, while Elene does not drop out of the story, she ceases to be the main character. After she overcomes Judas, although she is the inciting force of what follows, she takes a secondary place while Judas becomes without doubt the main character in the action.

In the *Andreas* the introduction informs us of the time and the place of the action, brings forth the main characters, suggests the mood of the whole, and sets before us clearly the action which precedes the main plot and is necessary for the understanding of it. Matthew has been condemned to death in the land of the cannibal Mermedonians. God promises to send Andrew to his aid. Then follows naturally the point of first interest where God commands Andrew to undertake the rescue. From this point we are held in suspense as to the outcome of Andrew's adventure.

But hardly has the action begun in the sea voyage, when the author drops the main thread of the plot and places before us the long, expository discourse of Andrew and the captain (469-817). This, as the account of the crimes of the devil in the *Juliana,* tends to dispel our interest in the main outcome of the story. It does serve to emphasize the strength and the faith of Andrew, but still it violates the unity of the whole, since such emphasis is unnecessary. Andrew's character is quite clear without it. A didactic digression of 349 lines in a poem of 1722 lines must be regarded as another instance of the lack of perspective common to Old English poetry.

Aside from this digression the main action of the poem is not seriously interrupted. It is delayed, however, by Andrew's narrative of his experience in the storm on the Sea of Galilee (429-460), by the description of the vision of Heaven (862-891), by the rather general beginning of the speech of God (925-935), and by a few of the author's comments on the action as in 1478-1491. Now these delays do not seriously violate the unity of the whole because they are brief. Moreover, Andrew's narrative of the storm on the sea serves to give verisimilitude to the voyage and to induce the men to sleep in order that the miraculous transportation to Mermedonia may be accomplished. The description of Heaven serves to convince Andrew of divine aid. And the beginning of God's speech is a natural introduction to what is to follow. The author's comments, of course, are not parts of the action of the story, but they are so brief that they may be disregarded. That is, we may conclude that the only serious violation of unity in the *Andreas* is the long discourse on the sea.

But we should notice that this poem is somewhat defective in a minor way from the point of view of unity in that parts of the action lack completeness and finality. Andrew arrives at Mermedonia with his band (843-849). During his experiences within the city there is no mention of his followers. At the end he appoints one Platan as bishop for the Mermedonians (1647-1654). Platan is probably one of Andrew's band. Presumably he has been patiently waiting outside of the city. Again, Matthew leads forth the prisoners (1044-1048). They are on a cannibal island. We hear not how they manage their departure thence. Finally, the story is defective in that the Mermedonians find it necessary to draw lots to determine which of their number is to suffer death to furnish food for the rest (1093-1103), when there are ready at hand the bodies of the slain guards (994-996).

In the *Christ* we may not look for the unity that lies in a single action with its beginning, its middle, and its end. Since the *Christ* is not narrative, since it does not arouse in us the feeling of suspense as to the event or outcome of the whole, we can look for the lyric unity alone. This is the unity of mood that is more easily felt than formulated. That the poem as a whole has this unity cannot be doubted. Its one predominating mood is the spirit of Advent, of the three-fold coming of Christ to men, through the Virgin birth, through the faith of the believer, and through the final judgment. That the general unity of the whole has not always been recognized, that the three main parts of the poem have been regarded as separate entities, can be due only to the fact that students have failed to recognize the existence or the force of that unity which is of mood alone.[2]

A detailed examination of the poem reveals nothing which does not bear directly upon the theme of the whole. Yet, since the unity is one of mood, since the appeal of the lyric is an emotional appeal, we must add that those parts of the poem which are manifestly expository, which appeal primarily to the intellect, do not contribute to the effect of the whole and violate the principle of lyric unity.

---

[2] I am not attempting to prove that the poem does not show traces of different hands. Differences in style may be due to copyists. The general unity of tone is manifest.

These expository passages occur first, as brief conclusions or moral interpretations added to emphasize the religious teaching that should follow from the emotional appeal. At the close of the passage which appeals to God to bestow light upon mankind, the author adds,

> Wē þæs þonc magon
> secgan Sigedryhtne   symle bi gewyrhtum,
> þæs þe hē hine sylfne ūs   sendan wolde.   (127-129)[3]

In these cases the explanatory additions are so brief and so nicely fitted into their places that the poem is not encumbered by them. They would perhaps not strike the general reader as added morals, since they are properly subordinated. However, in other cases, we have the direct, manifest addition of long morals or expository lessons. These should be omitted as they encumber the poem with explanatory statements of attitudes of the mind which result directly and poignantly from the emotional appeals.

The most striking instance begins with l. 586,—

> Hwæt! wē nū gehȳrdan   hū þæt Hǣlubearn
> þurh his hydercyme   hāls eft forgeaf,

and ends with l. 796,—

> Ic þæs brōgan sceal
> gesēon synwræce,   þæs þe ic sōð talge,
> þær monig[e] bēoð   on gemōt lǣded
> fore onsȳne   ēces Dēman.

and continues after the runic passage from 815 to 831.[4]

Lines 586-796 and 815-831 explain didactically the meaning of Christ's coming, enumerate the gifts of the Lord, interpret the words of Job and of Solomon, and advise man to think upon the day of Judgment. They are in the manner of a sermon. They stand in the same relation to the whole poem as do the explanatory passages of the *Juliana* and the *Elene* to those poems.

The *Christ* manifests a lack of unity, again, in abrupt changes of style or method of presentation. The author deserves the greatest praise, as we shall have occasion to note later, for giving variety to his work. But this variety is attained at the expense

---

3 See also ll. 33-35; 241-243; 468-470; 1079-1080; 1365-1369; 1598-1602; 1629-1633.

4 See also ll. 416-439; 1301-1311; 1316-1326; 1578-1590.

of congruity in tone. There is no gradation in change of method in the *Christ*. We feel that we are entering upon something new; we lose the sense of continuity when we are confronted with an abrupt change of style. The most striking instance of this is at l. 164. The preceding section (130-163) is a supplication for salvation addressed to the God of Spirits. It closes with the words

<blockquote>
Þū in hēannissum
wunast wīdeferh   mid Wāldend Fæder.
</blockquote>

Then, with l. 164 begins the dramatic colloquy of Joseph and Mary.

<blockquote>
(Mary) Ealā Iōsēph mīn,   Iācōbes bearn,
   mǣg Dāuīdes   mǣran cyninges,
   nū þū frēode scealt   fæste gedǣlan
   ālǣtan lufan mīne!
</blockquote>

Here the change of form is altogether too abrupt to allow us to retain the impression of continuity without which the impression of unity is impossible. And at the conclusion of this section after the words of Mary,—

<blockquote>
sceolde wītedōm
in him sylfum bēon   sōðe gefylled.   (212-213)
</blockquote>

the manner of the poem changes again to the supplication beginning

<blockquote>
Ealā þū sōða   ond þū sibsuma
ealra cyninga Cyning   Crīst ælmihtig.   (214-215)
</blockquote>

We are prepared for the change from the impassioned supplications of Part I to the narrative of Christ's ascension in the beginning of Part II, because the close of the first part marks in itself the conclusion of one distinct division of the poem. And after the narrative of Part II follows naturally the emotional effect of it, —

<blockquote>
Hwæt! wē nū gehȳrdan   hū þæt Hǣlubearn
þurh his hydercyme   hāls eft forgeaf,
.   .   .   .
.   .   .   .   Wuldor þæs āge
Þrȳnysse þrym,   þonc būtan ende!   (586-599)
</blockquote>

But with l. 600, the form changes abruptly to that of rather flat exposition,—

<blockquote>
Ðæt is þæs wyrðe   þætte werþēode
secgen Dryhtne þonc   duguða gehwylcre
þe ūs sīð ond ǣr   simle gefremede
þurh monigfealdra   mægna gerȳno.
</blockquote>

This same sort of abrupt change appears again in the insertion of the highly emotional runic passage (797-814), in the exposition which precedes and follows it and in the insertion of the expository passage (1578-1590) in the description of the Day of Doom.

Thus, while the *Christ* has a distinct unity of mood, in details it violates the principles of unity in the introduction of expository material which is not in tone with the general mood, and in the abrupt changes of form or method, which tend to destroy the effect of sequence. Moreover, the feeling of a lack of unity is occasioned by the lack of a definite order or arrangement of material. This fault we shall discuss later as it is particularly a fault in coherence.

In the *Juliana*, in the *Elene* within the primary and the secondary plot, and in the *Andreas* the principle of emphasis or mass is well followed in so far as it concerns the positions of the events of the stories.

The objective point of the plot of the *Juliana*, the deaths of the hero and heroine, comes at the end. The most important part of the story has the most emphatic position. Moreover, the different events of the story proceed from the beginning to the objective point in the order of climax. We have first the father's attempt to control Juliana and her delivery into the hands of Heliseus. Then we have the punishments inflicted by Heliseus in succession, each one stronger than the preceding. First, he offers her pardon, then he has her stripped and whipped, and finally he has her hung by the hair and scourged. After this comes to Juliana a more severe trial, the temptation of the devil. Now begins the new movement of the story. Juliana, with divine aid, binds the devil. Then, more important for the story, she remains unharmed in the two new tortures of Heliseus,—the fire in which he attempts to burn her is scattered and the molten lead into which she is to be cast is hurled back upon her torturers. Finally comes the objective point of the whole recital, the deaths of the two leading characters with the rewards of heaven and hell.

We need say little in regard to the emphasis of position in the *Elene*, since here, as in the *Juliana*, the events follow each other in the simple time order. The introduction unduly emphasizes

material which is not important for the story by giving it promi-
nence of position as well as of space. The same may be said of
the conclusions to the primary and the secondary plot. But a
most striking violation of the principle of emphasis of position
lies in the placing of the secondary plot, the unimportant part
of the story, in the most emphatic position. To the modern
reader this is disappointing. The main story stirs within us the
desire to know the outcome of the whole. With the discovery of
the true cross our desire is satisfied. What follows tends to
dissipate our interest, to leave most prominent in our minds the
secondary element. The finding of the nails might have been
used effectively as an incident leading up to the finding of the
cross. If it were made to precede the main event, it would retain
all of the interest which it has in itself, and it would also serve
to heighten the interest in the main event instead of to lessen it.

The objective point of the *Andreas*, the triumph of Andrew,
comes at the end. The most important incident has the most
emphatic position. The other incidents lead up to this objective
point in good order. We have first the introduction, then the
journey to Mermedonia, the release of Matthew, and the series
of tortures which lead to the objective point, Andrew's triumph.
After this follows the brief conclusion (1632-1722) telling of the
establishing of Christianity among the Mermedonians, which
serves to emphasize also the force of the triumph of Andrew.

Thus the emphasis of position is good. In fact, since, as in
the *Juliana* and the *Elene*, events proceed in the time order, there
was for the author no alternative.

In general the emphasis of position in the *Christ*, too, is good.
Part I deals with the least important phase of the subject, the
material coming of Christ, and Part III deals with the most
important, the Day of Doom. But in detail the emphasis of
position is not so good. We may see this in the fact that the
weaker, expository material in Part I holds the most emphatic
position at the close. But we must remember that to Cynewulf
probably the most didactic portion of his work was the most
important. That we do not have more of the intellectual, teaching element in the poem may be due not so much to the will of
the author as to the strength of his artistic instinct in spite of
that will.

Moreover, we must note that the long passage of exposition in Part II is inserted skilfully in the position where it will detract least from the whole. Had it been placed at the beginning, it might have condemned the poem to the lists of the unread; had it been placed at the end, it would have been emphasized unduly. As it stands, it comes into the poem after the mood of the reader has been attuned to the spirit of the whole and has been roused to a desire to proceed to the end. It immediately follows the narrative of Christ's ascension, in which the reader's interest is strong, and it contains the runic passage, which must have been specially attractive. The passages of exposition in the Christ, in themselves violating the principle of emphasis, stand, with the exception of the conclusion of Part I, in the positions in which they detract least from the effect of the whole.

In the poems which we are studying, while the emphasis of position is in general good, the emphasis of space is anything but good.

In the *Juliana* the actions of the story proceed in the order of climax; but the increasing importance of those actions is not made effective by the space allotted to them. This is especially true of the successive happenings from Heliseus' offer of pardon to the deaths of the main actors. And the insertion of the long recital of the devil, which forms one-third of the whole, is a most manifest violation of the principle of space emphasis. This recital is a digression. However, the space assigned to it makes this digression appear to be the main end of the story. The enveloping narrative becomes almost a mere frame employed to set off a tedious discourse on the temptations of the devil.

In the *Elene* the space given to the introduction and to the conclusion of the main plot of the story is out of proportion to the significance of those parts.

However, within the primary plot from the point of first interest to the final climax the space emphasis is in general good. After the point of first interest, the story progresses rapidly to the contest between Elene and the Jews. The author resists the natural Old English tendency, which we see in the *Andreas,* to dwell unduly upon the sea voyage. In fifty-five lines he trans-

ports Elene and her band over sea and land to the city of Jerusalem. Then, he passes briefly over the three assemblies of the
Jews, which are without direct result as far as Elene's object is
concerned, and takes up the speech of Judas, which has its importance in marking him as the agent through which Elene's
purpose is to be fulfilled. This speech has as much space as the
three fruitless assemblies together.

It is an essential step in the progress of the story; but it is
not so important as the following scene between Elene and Judas,
which is given less space. Then the fourth assembly, which only
leads to the selection of Judas as spokesman, is given space equal
to that of one of the other assemblies. Now we have an important
step, the forcing of Judas to disclose the cross, duly emphasized
with one hundred and eleven lines, and most important of all, the
actual discovery of the crosses, with one hundred and thirty-
eight lines. Finally, the miracle which discloses the true cross is
given briefly.

The emphasis of the story as manifested in the space assigned
to the main plot and to the secondary is again without fault.
To show that the secondary plot is regarded unquestionably as
secondary we have merely to note that the account of the finding
of the nails with its long conclusion takes up only about one
hundred and thirty lines.

In the *Andreas* the long digressive discourse on the sea is out
of all proportion when we consider the poem as a work of art.
And the recital of Andrew's experiences on the Sea of Galilee,
the description of Heaven, and some of the speeches and prayers
are also unduly emphasized. So also, the scene in which Andrew
is taken aboard the ship is given more space than its import for
the story as a whole warrants. All of these combine to delay the
rising movement by emphasizing unduly what is either useless or
not of vital importance for the event of the whole. As in the
Juliana, although not to so great a degree, we feel that the
author's zeal for religion was too strong, his regard for the art
of narration too conditional. This is manifest again in the space
assigned to the release of Matthew and to the concluding account
of the establishing of Christianity among the Mermedonians.
We should expect less space here and more in the scenes of the

DISCARDED

central and final climaxes. But in spite of the undue emphasis upon certain parts of the story on account of the author's religious purpose, in the *Andreas* we never for a moment feel that the story has become a mere setting for the exposition, as we do in the *Juliana*.

Of the three phases of the Advent spirit, which we noted in studying the unity of the *Christ*, the most important was the coming of God at the Day of Doom and the least important the coming of Christ in the flesh. The author implies this in the general apportionment of space in the poem. Part III, which deals exclusively with the Day of Doom, has 798 lines; Part II, which deals largely with the coming of the spirit of Christ to the individual, has 427 lines; and Part I, which deals both with the material and the spiritual coming of Christ, has 439 lines.[5]

Thus Cynewulf gives space to the three phases of his subject according to their importance. The space emphasis in detail is not so good. This is already clear from what we have noted in studying the unity of the poem. The introduction of didactic material, which violates the principle of unity, also violates the principle of emphasis in giving undue space to what is not an essential part of the whole.

The plots of the *Juliana*, the *Elene*, and the *Andreas* show manifest violations of the principles of unity and emphasis. But each poem shows a strict coherence in the general order of its parts. There are no overlappings of events, no synchronous actions. The material is arranged chronologically in what purports to be the actual order of the happenings. The *Andreas* contains the only instance of an abrupt change of scene at l. 167, where we drop the account of Matthew in Mermedonia and take up that of Andrew in Achaia. However, the connection between the two scenes is very close and very evident.

Then each poem has the virtue of introducing that part which is not in unity with the rest and not restricted to the space due to it in a natural and effective manner. For example, Andrew and his men are on the sea voyage which is to last the whole day. The storm has been stilled. All are asleep except Andrew and the pilot. Their conversation leads naturally to the subject of

---

[5] Some lines are lost at the beginning of the poem.

the Lord's power and the account of Christ's miracles. At length
Andrew falls asleep; and the main action begins again with his
transportation to Mermedonia.

The coherence of the plot of the *Juliana* in the sense of the
inner, logical connection between its parts is good. After the
situation at the beginning each event follows necessarily, causally
from what has preceded.

The death of Heliseus, which follows that of Juliana, is caused
by the execution of the maid. This, however, and the appearance
of the devil and the intervention of God in scattering the fire,
while they have their causes in what precedes, do not strike us
as necessary results. The intervention of superhuman powers as
the result of human actions partakes of the character of chance,
and is weak. But we must keep in mind the fact that the
intervention of divine powers in human affairs was to men of
Cynewulf's time not at all improbable. We must regard superhuman results as natural and necessary consequences when we
are dealing with a poem written for those to whose minds superhuman results were natural and necessary consequences.

Not so strong is the inner, causal relation between the parts
of the *Elene*. There is no sufficient cause for the summoning of
the three councils of the Jews. The digression which manifests
the strength of Judas against the devil is not a necessary result
of what precedes and it is not intimately related to what follows.
And the secondary plot has only a very weak causal relation to
the main plot. The successful termination of the search for the
cross leads Elene to desire to obtain the nails also. The posses-
sion of the nails leads her to seek the wise man whose words
bring about the fabrication of the wonderful bridle.

Throughout the *Andreas* we have what is impossible or improbable in the relations of events made probable and natural by
the situation at the beginning,—events are to be determined by
a superhuman power. Thus the element of chance is eliminated.
Andrew finds a ship waiting for him not by chance but by the
direct act of God. Actions do not proceed from human causes.
Andrew is made invisible, the guards fall dead, the swords melt.
etc., because God intervenes to control the progress of events.
But all of this is consistent with the supposition at the begin-

ning. For the men for whom the story was written, there was not even required that mental adjustment which we assume in reading stories of the marvelous. To primitive Christians the direct intervention of God in human affairs was a fact. For them and for us, when we have adjusted our minds to the situation at the beginning, the coherence of the story, in the sense of the inner, causal relation between its parts, is good with one exception. Andrew falls into the power of the Mermedonians not through their desire for vengeance but through the will of God. His sufferings are very edifying indeed and excellently foreshadowed, but they do not strike us as a necessary result of what has preceded or as a necessary cause for what is to follow. The strength of Andrew and the cruelty of the Mermedonians need no emphasis. The wonderful courage of the hero and the miraculous healing have no effect on the cannibals. The final triumph of the cause of Christianity is brought about by the flood alone.

In discussing the unity of the *Christ* we noted certain abrupt changes of form which destroyed the feeling of sequence. In these abrupt changes we have a striking violation of the principle of coherence. We have the introduction of a new style of expression which does not appear manifestly to be related to what immediately precedes it.

When we examine the poem in detail, we find that the coherence is excellent within each of the Twelve divisions of Part I. Take ll. 18-49. We have first the address,

> Ealā þū Reccend   ond þū riht Cyning—
> se þe locan healdeð,   līf ontȳneð—   (18-19)

then the request,

> ēadga ūs siges,   ōþrum forwyrned   (20)

and then the prayer in more detail,

> Hūru wē for þearfe   þās word sprecað,
> .   .   .   .
> .   .   .   .   (22-32)

The mention in the prayer of the saving power of the Lord, of the admission of the wretched to glory, leads to the observation,

> Forþon secgan mæg   sē ðe sōð spriceð
> þæt hē āhredde,   þā forhwyrfed wæs,
> frumcyn fīra.   (33-35)

Following this we have the manner of the saving,

> Wæs sēo fǣmne geong,
>
> . . . .
>
> . . . .   (35-41)

and the result of it,

> Eal giofu gǣstlīc   grundscēat geondsprēot;
>
> . . . .
>
> . . . .   (42-49)

This close coherence is a characteristic of all of the smaller divisions of Part I. The same holds true of the divisions of Part II and of Part III. At the beginning of Part II we have the narrative of the Ascension. Christ delivers his final message to his followers (476-490). Then He ascends to meet the heavenly messengers (491-510). In due order follow the words of the angels (510-526), the disappearance of the Lord (527-532), and the departure of the disciples to Jerusalem (533-545).

Again, take the beginning of Part III. First we have the introductory statement that the great Day of Doom shall come suddenly upon men as a thief in the night (867-874). This is followed by the more detailed picture,—

1. The summoning of all mankind by the trumpets of the angels. 875-889

2. The assembling of the good and the evil. 889-898.

3. The appearance of Christ in the assembly, gentle toward the good, bitter toward the wicked. 899-909

4. Christ's attitude toward the good. 910-917

5. Christ's attitude toward the wicked. 918-920

That is, the author of the *Christ* shows the ability to conceive the smaller scene as a whole with the proper relation of its parts. Now, when we turn to the larger scale, we see forthwith that he does not show the ability to view the smaller scenes as related parts of a larger whole. A cursory examination shows that Part I is a series of lyric outbursts thrown together at random. The successive passages begin as follows,—

1. (First lines lost.)
2. Ealā þū Reccend   ond þū riht Cyning,   18
3. Ealā sibbe gesihð,   sancta Hierūsalēm,   50
4. Ealā wīfa wynn,   71
5. Ealā Earendel,   engla beorhtast,   104
6. Ealā gǣsta God,   130

7. Ealā Iōsēph mīn,   164
8. Ealā þū sōða   ond þū sibsuma,
   ealra cyninga Cyning,   Crīst ælmihtig,   214-215
9. Ealā þū mæra   middangeardes,
   sēo clæneste   cwēn ofer eorþan,   275-276
10. Ealā þū hālga   heofona Dryhten,   348
11. Ealā sēo wlitige,   weorðmynda full,
    hēah ond hālig,   heofoncund Þrȳnes,   378-379.
12. Ealā! hwæt þæt is wræclīc wrixl,   416

The fourth division and the ninth are addressed directly to the Virgin Mary. Between them the fifth, sixth, and eighth are addressed to Christ, while the seventh is the colloquy of Joseph and Mary. The third addresses the Holy Jerusalem, and the eleventh the Trinity. Moreover, the divisions are not arranged as they have to do with the material coming of Christ or the spiritual. The first, fifth, eighth, and eleventh refer specially to the spiritual coming. Such arrangement could have been determined by nothing but chance.

Part I, then, shows an absolute lack of the sense for larger coherence, of the restraint in the midst of lyric fervor which determines the structural plan of the whole.

Part II shows a much stronger coherence. It consists of two main divisions, the narrative of the Ascension and the lesson to be drawn from the Ascension. The first division (440-585) is in itself coherent. It is true that the speech which begins at l. 558 marks a clear break as it is printed. If, however, we follow Cook in interpreting this as a continuation of the speech which closes with l. 526,[6] we may conclude that the lack of coherence here is due to an error of a copyist.

At the beginning of the second division the author summarizes the narrative,—

> Hwæt! wē nū gehȳrdan   hū þæt Hǣlubearn
> þurh his hydercyme   hāls eft forgeaf.   (586-587)

and draws the conclusion,—

> Wuldor þæs āge
> Þrȳnysse þrym,   þonc būtan ende!
> Ðæt is þæs wyrðe   þætte werþēode
> secgen Dryhtne þonc   duguða gehwylcre.   (598-601)

Then he enumerates the blessings of the Lord, gives the testimony of Job and of Solomon concerning the greatest of these, the

---

6 *The Christ of Cynewulf*, pp. 129-131.

Ascension, exhorts us to strive to attain that final blessing, and warns us of the doom of those who do not attain it. In this division the *Christ* shows the lack of coherence which is common in Old English poetry, the forward and backward movement caused by the overlapping of material. Everything leads naturally to the enumeration of the gifts of the Lord, which is concluded with l. 632. Following this naturally is the testimony of Job and the prophet concerning the greatest of these gifts (633-658). We feel that we have done with the blessings of the Lord. But not so. The author goes back on his tracks to enumerate still more of the gifts which God has conferred upon man (659-685).

Then he mentions the Lord's blessings upon the angels and His honor upon His handiwork. He interprets the lights of the sky as the shining church of God triumphing through the Ascension (686-711). The mention of the triumph of the Ascension turns the author back rather mechanically to Solomon's song of the six leaps of the Lord (712-743) and to the lessons to be drawn from it (744-866).

From the structure of Part II, again, we must conclude that Cynewulf lacked the sense for the coherence between the parts of the larger whole; for, while this part does show a logical arrangement in the division into the narrative of the Ascension and the lesson to be drawn from it, that division is so natural as to require no special ability. And, moreover, within the second division the coherence is marred by the faulty overlapping of parts.

Part III, too, shows a lack of coherence in the inability of the poet to keep the larger scene before him as a whole. As we have seen, he presents first a coherent picture of the summoning of mankind, the appearance of God, and the attitude of the Lord towards the hosts come to judgment. Then he draws the conclusion, "Let this be a lesson to teach man to prepare to meet God," (920-929). Then he begins over again to picture the coming of the Day of Doom:—

Fires shall consume the earth, the sun shall become dark, and the moon and the stars shall fall headlong. 930-940

God shall visit all quarters of the earth with an all-consuming fire, which shall embrace ocean, land, and sky. 941-971

Fire shall consume all creatures of earth and sea. 972-1006

God shall come to the mount and all men who have inhabited the earth shall appear before Him in their true light. 1007-1042

Fire shall embrace the earth and the stars shall fall. All souls shall come to judgment where naught may be concealed. 1047-1060.

All men shall be summoned to judgment. Glorious shall it be for the sinless, most sad for the sinful. Sinners shall behold Christ on the cross and realize the crime of the crucifixion. Sad shall it be for them to look upon the suffering of the Lord. 1061-1215.

Lines 930-1215 cover with new details the same ground as lines 867-874. And within the second picture also we have this same overlapping. Here are four descriptions of the all-consuming fires (930-940; 941-971; 972-1006; 1039-1044) presented as if they were pictures of succeeding scenes instead of the same.

The last part of the poem (1216-1664) beginning with the description of the judgment shows a more distinct progress and a more orderly arrangement of material. First we have the separation of the chosen onés from the sinners and the three signs visible to each group (1216-1311). Then follows the lesson, "Let each one look into his heart" (1312-1333). Next we have the words of the Judge, first, to the blessed and second, to the damned (1334-1523). After these words the damned are consigned to Hell (1524-1548). Then, again, follows the lesson, "The doom of the sinner should make us look to our deeds in the flesh" (1549-1590). And finally there are the concluding descriptions of the torments of Hell and of the joys of Heaven (1591-1664). But here, too, we have the coherence marred by didactic interpolations (1312-1333; 1549-1590) and by the repetition of the description of the torments of Hell (1524-1548; 1591-1633).

We have seen that the *Christ* shows a strict coherence within the limits of the smaller divisions in each of its three main parts. We have seen that it shows a distinct lack of coherence in the relations between the divisions within each of its main parts. Finally, let us notice the relation between the three main parts.

That this is not so close as it might be is evident from the fact that the three parts of the *Christ* have been regarded as three independent poems.

These three parts, as we have already noted, are closely connected by their mood, by the fundamental conception of the coming of Christ. But each part does not treat a distinct, necessary phase of that coming. Part I deals with Christ's coming in the flesh and His coming to the soul of the believer. Part II draws from the Ascension the lessons of His coming to the soul of the believer and His coming to the individual at death. Part III deals exclusively with His coming to judge mankind. Part I does not point forward to the Ascension or to the Doomsday. Part II begins as a new poem. Its relation to Part I must be felt by the reader. We have nowhere in the text of Part I the statement or the hint that other phases of the Advent spirit are to be presented. In Part II, however, we have references to the nativity (444 ff; 587; 628; 720 ff; 786 ff).[7]

These do not imply necessarily that they are direct references to what has gone before. We have also in Part II references to the Doomsday:

> wile eft swā-þēah   eorðan mægðe
> sylfa gesēcan   sīde herge,
> ond þonne gedēman   dǣda gehwylce
> þāra ðe gefremedon   folc under roderum.   (523-526)

and the conclusion of this part (782-866). The first of these might well be due to chance, but the second is undoubtedly looking forward to Part III, as it contains several of the distinctive features of the Judgment as it is there pictured.[8]

And since Part III also contains a reference to the Nativity:

> þā ic sylf gestāg,
> māga in mōdor,   þēah wæs hyre mægdenhād
> ǣghwæs onwālg.   .   .   .   .   .   (1418 ff)

we should probably be correct in regarding the references to the Nativity in Part II as intentional references to the material which precedes. However, in spite of this, the connection between Part I and Part II is not strong, because the end of I does not direct us to the beginning of II as does the end of II to the

---

[7] Noted by Cook, *The Christ of Cynewulf*, Introd., p. xxii.

[8] See Cook, *The Christ of Cynewulf*, Introd., p. xxii.

beginning of III. Here, again, in the relation between the main parts we find evidence for our conviction that Cynewulf does not show the power of seeing his whole work in perspective, of handling adequately the architectonics of the poem as a unit.

COMPARISON WITH THE BEOWULF AND WITH THE LATIN.

Up to this point our study of the plots of the *Juliana,* the *Elene,* and the *Andreas* has shown in general that each of these stories embodies one unified action; that the unity of the whole is weakened by the inclusion of digressive or episodic matter which is aside from the one unified action; and that this inclusion of digressive matter destroys the emphasis or mass of the whole. Now, when we turn to the heroic epic for comparison, we find that the plot of the *Beowulf* shows a well-defined main action, with its beginning, the determination of Beowulf to conquer Grendel, its middle, the destruction of Grendel, and its end, the destruction of Grendel's mother. But this is not all of the story. Beowulf, the hero, returns to his own land, becomes king of the Geats, and rules for fifty years. Then we have a second story with its beginning, Beowulf's determination to slay the dragon, its middle, the fight with the dragon, and its end, the deaths of the dragon and Beowulf. The two stories, each a unit in itself, are connected only by the fact that the same man is the hero throughout.

In limiting the story to a single main action or to a series of actions causally related, the *Juliana,* the *Elene,* and the *Andreas* mark an advance upon the *Beowulf* in narrative method. Primitive narratives which furnish the material for epics tend to include many actions connected merely by that fact that one man is the hero in all. In this form is the *Gest of Robin Hood,* which, half as long as the *Beowulf,* has twice as many incidents.[9] The *Beowulf,* then, represents an artistic development higher than that of the ballad cycle, since it narrows its plot to two main actions; and the *Juliana,* the *Elene,* and the *Andreas* represent an artistic development higher than that of the *Beowulf,* since they narrow their plots to one main action each.

---

[9] Hart, *Ballad and Epic,* pp. 91-92; 185.

To account for the narrowing of the number of actions in the Christian epics it is not necessary to refer to any foreign influence. We have a natural development of narrative form from the ballad cycle, through the *Beowulf* to the Christian epic. We should add, however, that this natural tendency to lessen the number of actions was emphasized by the influence of the Latin. And for this influence we need not look to the Latin poems. The confirming influence toward lessening the number of actions lay in the Latin or Greek legends of saints which were the direct sources of the Old English religious epics.

Again, the characteristic digressions which destroy the unity of the *Juliana,* the *Elene,* and the *Andreas* may be accounted for by the influence of earlier Old English poems such as the *Beowulf.*. The *Beowulf* shows the tendency to depart from the main line of action in the account of the swimming match (499-589), in the accounts of Sigemund and of Finn and Hnæf (874-900; 1068-1159), in the moralizings of Hrothgar (1651-1919), and in the observations and reminiscences of Beowulf (2020-2069; 2425-2509). Here, too, the Christian epics show an advance upon the *Beowulf* in including less of episodic or digressive material. There is the same tendency of the more advanced narrative to limit the number of actions. But the Latin or Greek prose legends which were used as sources of the Old English poems, were here, too, a confirming influence. The *Acta S. Julianae,* Caput II, 7-11,[10] contains the same digressive discourse of the devil that we find in the Old English. The digressive part of the speech of Judas in the *Elene* finds its source in the Latin *Vita Quiriaci* in the *Acta Sanctorum* of the fourth of May.[11]

The *Christ,* as we have seen, stands apart from the other poems in that it is lyric and didactic. Its unity is that of mood. It is made up loosely of three main parts, which treat different phases of its fundamental conception. It is weakened by much exposition, by abrupt changes of style, and by the lack of a definite order or arrangement of material. Its general form,

---

[10] As published by Bolland, *Acta Sanctorum,* Feb., tom. ii, pp. 875-879 (Feb. 16). Reprinted in Strunk's *Juliana,* pp. 33-49.

[11] See Kent, *Cynewulf's Elene,* pp. 34-39.

distinct from that of the *Juliana*, the *Elene*, and the *Andreas*, cannot be accounted for by the influence of such poems as the *Beowulf*.

Is the form of the *Christ*, then, original with Cynewulf or is it due to the influence of the Latin? In the first place, there is nothing similar to the form of the *Christ* in the Latin prose legends of the saints. But in the medieval Latin poems we find forms which may have influenced Cynewulf. The *Carmen Paschale* of Sedulius[12] is a poem of Christ Our Passover in five books. The first book takes up the miraculous deliverances of the Old Testament, the second takes up the birth and childhood of Christ, and the third, fourth, and fifth take up the great saving *miracula Christi* until the final paschal sacrifice and redemption, consisting of Christ's death, resurrection, manifestation of Himself, and His Ascension.[13]

De spiritalis historiae gestis of Avitus, written in the first quarter of the sixth century, is again a poem made up of a number of divisions: *De origine mundi, De originali peccato, De sententia dei, De diluvio mundi*, and *De transitu maris rubri*. The first three of these have a definite subject in the fall of man.[14]

Such poems may have been a force in determining the form of the *Christ* with its three loosely connected divisions. And the *Alethia*, commentaries on Genesis, by Claudius Marius Victor, from about the middle of the fifth century, an expository rendering of the Biblical story of Genesis, with many didactic digressions,[15] and similar poems may have been a force in causing Cynewulf to include much didactic material in the *Christ*.

But we can better account for the form of the *Christ* by material that was much nearer to Cynewulf and much more familiar. The division of the *Christ* into three main parts was probably due to the church's recognition of a three-fold advent of Christ. St. Bernard, in his third Advent Sermon, says,

---

12 *Corpus Scriptorum Ecclesiasticorum Latinorum*, v. X, pp. 14-146.

13 Taylor, *The Classical Heritage of the Middle Ages*, pp. 281-82.

14 Migne, *Patrologiae Cursus Completus*, series Latina Prior, v. 59, pp. 323-382. Taylor, p. 282.

15 Taylor, p. 281.

"Triplicem enim ejus adventum novimus: ad homines, in homines, contra homines."[16]

The lyric element in the *Christ* is accounted for by the Latin sources of parts of the poem. Part I is a modification of the Antiphons of the church service, such as,—

O rex gentium, et desideratus earum, lapisque angularis, qui facis utraque unum: veni, et salva hominem, quem de limo formasti.[17]

Part II derives much of its lyric element from the Ascension hymn ascribed to Bede, beginning,

> Hymnum canamus gloriae,
> hymni novi nunc personent;
> Christus novo cum tramite
> ad Patris ascendit thronum.[18]

And Part III has much of the descriptive and didactic elements of such hymns as the one beginning,

> Apparebit repentina dies magna Domini,
> fur obscura velut nocte improvisos occupans.[19]

Finally, for the abundant exposition which is mixed with the lyrical passages of the *Christ*, we need only look to the homilies of the early church, such as the Ascension sermon of Pope Gregory the Great.[20]

Thus we find the general form of the *Christ* due to the influence of the Antiphons, hymns, and sermons of the early church. This influence did not bring about a modification of the old heroic epic, since the form of the latter was too firmly established to admit of vital modification. The influence of popular Latin poetry and prose gave to Old English poetry a new form. But we must remember that the metrical structure of the *Christ* is the same as that of the heroic epic and the religious narrative poems. And we must not be led to suppose that, since the general form of the *Christ* is due to the Latin of the church, the poem does not show in details correspondences with the *Beowulf* and with the *Juliana*, the *Elene*, and the *Andreas*. These we shall note in discussing the subject of methods of plot development.

---

[16] See Cook, Introd., xxvii-xxviii.

[17] Cook, Introd., xxxv-xliii, and pp. 71-73.

[18] Cook, pp. 116-118.

[19] Cook, pp. 171-172.

[20] Cook, Introd., xliii, and pp. 118-119.

V.

METHODS OF PLOT DEVELOPMENT.

We have examined the fundamental conception and the general form of the Christian epic, and we have studied in some detail the unity, emphasis, and coherence of plot. We turn now to the methods of development, to the forms or kinds of expression which are employed in the construction of the poems.

Aside from conversation or the reports of the direct words of the characters, the *Juliana*, the *Elene*, the *Andreas*, and the *Christ* are developed in the first place by simple objective narrative. By this I mean the mere recital of events, the statement of what happened, as it might be reported by a witness, exclusive of the mental action and the words of the actors. The following will serve to illustrate:

> Hȳ þā þurh yrre Affricanus
> fæder fǣmnan āgeaf on fēonda geweald
> Heliseo. Hē in ǣringe
> gelǣdan hēt æfter lēohtes cyme
> tō his dōmsetle. Duguð wāfade
> on þǣre fǣmnan wlite, folc ealgeador.
>
> *Juliana*, 158-163.

Of this objective narrative, aside from the few words introducing the speakers throughout the poem, the *Juliana* has in all about 180 lines.[1] The *Elene* has in all about 600 lines;[2] the *Andreas* about 575 lines;[3] and the *Christ* about 110 lines.[4]

---

[1] Lines 32-33; 41-45; 59-68; 158-165; 225-246; 530-538; 553-618; 635-640; 669-695. There are only two instances of indirect discourse, ll. 559-563; 573-580.

[2] Lines 18-39; 41-56; 65-78; 85-96; 99-162; 166-193; 198-210; 214-240; 243-246; 248-265; 271-287; 320-332; 377-385; 411-419; 547-551; 555-573; 585-588; 598-605; 609-610; 691-698; 709-725; 803-807; 828-837; 843-852; 860-893; 895-896; 897-902; 935-939; 968-1027; 1033-1073; 1094-1120; 1126-1167; 1197-1229. There is one instance of indirect discourse (667-668) and one instance of the mixture of direct and indirect (157-165) which is common in early Germanic literature.

[3] Lines 40-51; 59-62; 88-96; 118-120; 125-128; 167-173; 225-231; 235-238; 239-241; 244-255; 349-354; 359-360; 364-369; 382-385; 401-404; 461-465; 467-470; 818-836; 843-850; 910-913; 977-979; 981-1023; 1026-1150; 1155-1163; 1168-1172; 1201-1207; 1219-1255; 1269-1280; 1296-1299; 1307-1315; 1334-1342; 1386-1400; 1446-1450; 1455-1467; 1469-1477; 1492-1497; 1522-1557; 1569-1601; 1613-1663; 1675-1677; 1695-1716. There are instances of indirect discourse in 1080-1085; 1108-1111.

[4] Lines 87-88; 195-196; 224-229; 233-238; 460-467; 470-475; 502-510; 527-537; 540-557; 1027-1038; 1334-1343; 1362-1364; 1370-1378; 1515-1518; 1524-1526. These passages contain a few lines of subjective narrative, but it is manifestly subordinate. We should note, too, that the narrative interest

In the second place the poems are developed by subjective narrative, the report of how external actions affect the mind of a character, the inner mental action which would be manifest to a witness only in its external results, as in

> Hwæðre hē in brēostum þā gīt
> herede in heortan   heofonrīces weard,
> þēah ðe hē ātres drync   atulne onfēnge;
> ēadig ond onmōd   hē mid elne forð
> wyrðode wordum   wuldres aldor,
> heofonrīces weard,   hālgan stefne,
> of carcerne;   him wæs Crīstes lof
> on fyrhðlocan   fæste bewunden.
>
> *Andreas*, 51-58.

The *Juliana* contains only a few lines of subjective narrative;[5] the *Elene* contains about 60 lines;[6] the *Andreas* about 75 lines;[7] and the *Christ* only about 10 lines.[8]

The *Juliana* contains almost no description for its own sake. We have the explanatory description of Maximian and his reign (ll. 1-17) and of Heliseus (18-26), which gives necessary information at the beginning of the story. But, aside from this, the characters are described only by a line here and there or by an epithet. And direct descriptions of background are limited to a few words. Moreover, there is very little concrete detail in the pictures presented by the narrative. The only approach to the concrete method of narration which we shall find in the *Elene* is the account of the vessel of molten lead:

> Næs se fēond tō læt,
> sē hine gelærde   þæt hē læmen fæt
> biwyrcan hēt   wundorcræfte,
> wīges wōmum   ond wudubēamum,
> holte bi[h]lænan.   Ðā sē [hearda] bibēad
> þæt mon þæt lāmfæt   lēades gefylde,
> ond þā onbærnan hēt   bælfīra mæst,
> ād onælan;   sē wæs æghwonan
> ymbboren mid brondum;   bæð hāte wēol.   (573-581)

---

is strong in other passages which we may term more concrete narrative or description as we will. In this objective narrative we have indirect discourse in ll. 449-453; 547-550. Indirect discourse is also found in ll. 204-206; 282-286; 301-305; 691-694; 1549-1554.

    [5] Lines 26-31; 33-41; 58-59. There are throughout the poem other brief references to the effects of action upon the minds of the characters.

    [6] Lines 40-41; 56-65; 96-98; 194-197; 212-214; 246-247; 266-271; 584-585; 627-631; 840-843; 953-967.

    [7] Lines 51-58; 122-123; 129-156; 160-167; 231-234; 260-263; 376-381; 892-896; 1262-1269.

    [8] Lines 499-502; 537-540; 1103-1106.

In the *Elene* direct description of the individual characters and of the scene of the action is limited for the most part to a qualifying word or phrase. The only direct description of char-acter of more than a line or two is the introduction to the poem, which describes the character of Constantine (1-18). Direct description of the background or scene of the action is so inter-woven with the action itself that the two are not distinct. Parts of the poem which contain such passages as,—

	Fyrdlēoð āgōl
wulf on wealde,	wælrūne ne māð:
ūrigfeðera earn	sang āhōf
lāðum on lāste.	(27-30)

the account of the battle (109-126), of the sea voyage (232-246), and of the landing of Elene's band (248-265) show the author's more concrete style of narration rather than the use of descrip-tion for the setting or for the suggestion of mood apart from the narrative.[9] For this concrete method of narration, for the intro-duction of the distinctive details of a picture in the manner in which they are observed in life, for the blending of description into the body of the narrative, Cynewulf deserves the highest praise.

The *Andreas* contains 38 lines of pure description[10] which places before us the scene in which the action takes place. We have not merely the vivid details of the action itself, as in the *Elene*, but the frame which sets off the picture of the action. The following passage will serve to illustrate this,—

Gewāt him þā on uhtan   mid ærdæge
ofer sandhleoðu   tō sǣs waruðe,
þrīste on geþance,   ond his þegnas mid,
gangan on grēote;   gārsecg hlynede,
bēoton brimstrēamas.   Se beorn wæs on hyhte,
syðþan hē on waruðe   wīdfæðme scip
mōdig gemētte.   þā cōm morgentorht
bēacna beorhtost   ofer breomo snēowan,
hālig of heolstre;   heofoncandel blāc
ofer lagoflōdas.   (235-244)

The distinctly descriptive character of *gārsecg hlynede*, *bēoton brimstrēamas*, and *þā cōm morgentorht* . . . . *ofer*

---

9 See also ll. 23-25; 50-56; 226-228; 1110-1116.
10 Lines 123-125; 238-239; 241-244; 369-376; 465-467; 836-843; 1255-1262; 1305-1306.

lagoflōdas, in the midst of very specific narrative, may be seen from the fact that these lines may be omitted without destroying the sequence of the narrative proper.

Then the *Andreas* contains one instance of general description in the opening lines of the poem. In lines 1-11 we have not the description of a particular person or of a particular scene, but a general characterization of the twelve apostles; we have a description not of their action in any one instance but of their action in general.

We have also about 55 lines of general narration,[11] as in

> Swylc wæs þæs folces   freoðoléas tācen,
> unlǣdra eafoð,   þæt hīe ēagena gesihð,
> hettend heorogrimme,   hēafodgimmas,
> āgētton gealgmōde   gāra ordum.
> Syððan him geblēndan   bitere tōsomne,
> drȳas þurh dwolcræft,   drync unhēorne,
> sē onwende gewit,   wera ingeþanc,
> heortan[on] hreðre.   (29-36)

Here the story is concerned with the actions of the Mermedonians in general, not in any one particular case.

The *Christ,* too, shows little description for its own sake. Direct description of character of more than a qualifying word or two is rare. We have

> Bið þonne rīces Weard   rēþe ond meahtig,
> yrre ond egesful.   Ondweard ne mæg
> on þissum foldwege   fēond gebīdan.   (1527-1529),

which is hardly to be distinguished from what we have termed subjective narrative. Then, we have the description of the Virgin,

> Wæs sēo fǣmne geong,
> .   .   .   .
> Nǣnig efenlīc þām,   ǣr nē siþþan,
> in worlde gewearð   wīfes g[e]ea[c]nung;
> þæt dēgol wæs   Dryhtnes gerȳne.   (35-41)

For descriptions of the scene of the action we are confined to the pictures of the Day of Doom, as in

> Dyneð dēop gesceaft,   ond fore Dryhtne fǣreð
> wælmfȳra mǣst   ofer wīdne grund,
> hlemmeð hāta lēg;   heofonas berstað;
> trume ond torhte   tungol ofhrēosað.   (930-933)

---

[11] Lines 11-39; 157-160; 1302-1305; 1677-1694.

Of this description, where the purpose seems to be the forma-
tion of an image without stirring our interest in the outcome of
the action, we have in all about one hundred lines.[12] But we have
other passages, especially in the treatment of the Day of Doom,
in which the elements of narration and description are so inter-
woven that we may term them description or, better probably,
very concrete, vivid narrative. Such is the picture of the
Ascension,—

> Đā wearð semninga   swēg on lyfte
> hlūd gehȳred;   heofonengla þrēat,
> weorud wlitescȳne,   wuldres āras,
> cwōmun on corðre.   Cyning ūre gewāt
> þurh þæs temples hrōf,   þǣr hȳ tō sēgun,—
> þā þe lēofes þā gēn   lāst weardedun
> on þām þingstede,   þegnas gecorene.   (491-497)

Such are many of the pictures of the Day of Doom, as

> Þonne heofon ond hel   hæleþa bearnum
> fīra fēorum   fylde weorþ[a]ð,
> Grundas swelgað   Godes ondsacan;
> lācende lēg   lāðwende men
> þrēað, þēodsceaþan,   ond nō þonan lǣt[e]ð
> on gefēan faran   tō feorhnere;
> ac se bryne bindeð   bīdfæstne here,
> fēoð firena bearn.   (1591-1598)

Of this blending of narration and description we have about 279
lines.[13]

Again, the *Juliana,* the *Elene,* and the *Andreas* have very
little comment on the action. In the *Juliana* the only reference
to the story-teller is in the pronoun *wē* which occurs in the
traditional formal phrase of the first line. The author of the
Elene comments on the action seven times.[14] In most cases the
religious fervor of the man causes him to emphasize the morals to
be drawn from the story by stating them. In the *Andreas* the
author appears a few times in the formal use of the pronoun in
the first person (1; 360; 1093; 1706). A few times he emphasizes
the religious significance of the action, as in 120-121. And he

---

[12] Lines 35-49; 797-814; 832-863; 930-940; 1021-1026; 1088-1089; 1527-
1529; 1649-1664.

[13] Lines 491-499; 867-920; 941-1014; 1039-1056; 1061-1079; 1107-1183;
1216-1300; 1530-1548; 1559-1577; 1591-1598; 1602-1629; 1634-1648.

[14] Lines 210-211; 240-242; 837-839; 893-894; 896; 1027-1033; 1229-1236.

delays once to state that it is beyond his power to tell adequately
the events of the life of Andrew (1478-1487)—the only instance
of such comment in these poems.

The fact that much of the *Christ* is subjective, while the
Juliana, the *Elene*, and the *Andreas* are largely objective, makes
the place of the author in this poem a prominent one. Throughout Part I the many supplications to God make the use of the
pronoun in the first person frequent. And in Part II and in
Part III, where we have some objective narration and description, the author makes himself felt in the many exhortations
addressed to his audience. Throughout the poem there is much
exposition in the author's comment on the action and in the
lessons which he wishes to teach from the Advent celebration.
His warm desire to turn men to God allows him to miss no
opportunity of bringing home to their intellects as well as to
their emotions the glory of the chosen ones and the torments of
the doomed. In all we have about 375 lines of exposition,—over
one-fifth of the whole.[15]

This exposition ranges from the passages where the appeal is
purely intellectual, as in

> Forþon secgan mæg　　sē ðe sōð spriceð
> þæt hē āhredde,　　þā forhwyrfed wæs,
> frumcyn fīra.　　(33-35)

to those where there is a large infusion of the emotional element,
although the primary appeal is still intellectual,—

> 　　　　　Ær sceal geþencan
> gæstes þearfe,　　se þe Gode mynteð
> bringan beorhtne wlite,　　þonne bryne costað,
> hāt, heorugīfre,　　hū gehealdne sind
> sāwle wið synnum　　fore Sigedēman.　　(1056-1060)

The emotional element increases in these passages until they
merge into what I have called lyric outbursts of exhortation.
These with the lyric outbursts of supplication and of praise are
forms of expression not found in the other poems except in the
few instances where the prayers or exhortations of the characters
are reported as such in direct discourse.

---

[15] Lines 33-35; 119-129; 135-146; 219-223; 241-243; 426-439; 468-470;
600-620; 627-650; 654-714; 720-771; 779-796; 921-929; 1015-1021; 1056-
1060; 1079-1080; 1081-1088; 1090-1102; 1183-1215; 1301-1311; 1316-1333;
1365-1369; 1549-1558; 1578-1590; 1598-1602; 1629-1633.

In what I have termed lyric outbursts of exhortation we find
an important expository element. But the appeal to the emotions
is stronger than that to the intellect. One example will suffice to
illustrate this,—

> Utan ūs beorgan þā,
> þenden wē on eorðan   eard weardigen!
> Utan ūs tō Fæder   freoþa wilnian,
> biddan Bearn Godes   ond þone blīðan Gǣst,
> þæt hē ūs gescilde   wið sceaþan wǣpnum,
> lāþra lygesearwum,   se ūs līf forgeaf,
> leomu, līc, ond gæst!   (771-777)[16]

These exhortations, as we have said, merge into the more
purely expository passages so that no hard and fast line can be
drawn between them. More distinct are the lyric outbursts of
supplication, as in

> Swā þū, God of Gode   gearo ācenned,
> Sunu sōþan Fæder,   swegles in wuldre
> būtan anginne   ǣfre wǣre,
> swā þec nū for þearfum   þīn āgen geweorc
> bideð þurh byldo   þæt þū þā beorhtan ūs
> sunnan onsende,   ond þē sylf cyme,
> þæt ðū inlēohte   þā þe longe ǣr
> þrosme beþeahte,   ond in þēostrum, hēr
> sǣton sinneahtes   synnum bifealdne,
> deorc dēaþes sceadu   drēogan sceoldan.   (109-118)[17]

Finally we have lyric outbursts of praise,—

> Ealā Earendel,   engla beorhtast
> ofer middangeard   monnum sended,
> ond sōðfæsta   sunnan lēoma,
> torht ofer tunglas,—   þū tīda gehwane
> of sylfum þē   symle inlīhtes.   (104-108)[18]

Altogether the *Christ* contains more than 325 lines of purely
lyric praise, supplication and exhortation.

Of all the methods of development in the *Juliana*, the *Elene*,
and the *Andreas* by far the most important is direct discourse.
Of the 695 lines of the *Juliana* (the author's personal epilogue
is not part of the story) about 450 lines are taken up by the

---

[16] See also ll. 440-460; 586-599; 815-831; 864-866.

[17] See also ll. 9-17; 18-23; 71-87; 243-274; 335-347; 358-377; 1312-1315.

[18] See also ll. 1-8; 50-70; 130-135; 214-218; 239-240; 275-316; 326-334;
348-358; 378-402; 416-425; 777-778.

direct speeches of the characters.[19] Five hundred and fifty of
the 1236 lines of the *Elene*[20] and 900 of the 1722 lines of the
Andreas[21] are direct discourse. And about 275 lines[22] or one-
sixth of the *Christ* are given to the speeches of the characters or
to the direct quotation of the words of authorities.

This direct discourse performs various functions. It serves
to impart to the reader general information,[23] to impart information essential to the full appreciation of the story,[24] to portray
character,[25] to summarize actions which have preceded those of
the main account,[26] to give verisimilitude or variety,[27] and to
lend authority to statements which are quoted.[28]

But the most important function of direct discourse is to
further the actions of the plot. Every important step in the
development of the story of the *Juliana* is brought about by the
speeches of its characters. Direct discourse is not employed so

[19] Lines 46-57; 68-77; 80-88; 93-104; 108-116; 119-129; 132-139; 144-
146; 149-157; 166-174; 176-183; 190-208; 210-224; 247-257; 261-267; 272-
282; 284-286; 289-315; 317-318; 321-344; 348-350; 352-428; 431-453; 456-
530; 539-553; 619-627; 632-634; 641-669.

[20] Lines 79-85; 162-165; 288-319; 333-376; 386-395; 397-403; 406-410;
419-535; 538-546; 551-554; 574-584; 588-597; 605-608; 611-618; 621-626;
632-641; 643-654; 656-661; 663-666; 670-682; 683-684; 686-690; 699-708;
726-802; 808-827; 853-859; 903-934; 940-953; 1074-1093; 1121-1125; 1168-
1196.

[21] Lines 63-87; 97-117; 174-188; 190-201; 203-224; 256-259; 264-269;
271-276; 279-284; 286-289; 292-298; 301-304; 307-314; 317-342; 344-348;
355-358; 386-395; 397-400; 405-414; 417-426; 429-460; 471-509; 511-536;
540-554; 557-571; 573-600; 603-616; 618-622; 624-627; 629-631; 633-642;
644-817; 851-856; 859-891; 897-909; 914-917; 920-924; 926-976; 1023-1025;
1164-1167; 1173-1183; 1185-1194; 1197-1200; 1208-1218; 1281-1295; 1300-
1301; 1316-1333; 1343-1344; 1347-1359; 1362-1374; 1376-1385; 1401-1428;
1431-1445; 1451-1454; 1467-1468; 1498-1521; 1558-1568; 1602-1606; 1609-
1612; 1664-1674; 1717-1722.

[22] Lines 89-103; 149-195; 197-213; 230-232; 317-325; 403-415; 476-490;
510-526; 558-585; 621-626; 651-653; 715-719; 1344-1361; 1379-1514; 1519-
1523.

[23] The conversation of the heroine and the devil (*Juliana*, 289-553)
imparts general information about the nature and the deeds of the devil.

[24] The speech of Judas (*Elene*, 726-802) informs us that the finding of
the cross will be fatal to the religion of the Jews.

[25] The description of heaven (*Andreas*, 859-891) shows the glory of the
character of Andrew.

[26] The speeches of God in judging man (*Christ*, 1344-1361; 1379-1514)
summarize the acts which have led to the doom of the wicked.

[27] The words of the Mermedonians (*Andreas*, 1717-1722) serve primarily
to give verisimilitude to the close of the poem.

[28] God's own words (*Christ*, 230-232) are quoted to emphasize the statement of the author.

exclusively in the *Elene*. Yet we have the direct words of Elene and the Jews (286-410; 573-597) and of Judas and the Jews (417-547) in the situations which lead up to the crisis of the poem. The scene which contains the crisis (604-708), where Elene forces Judas to disclose the cross, is developed by dramatic conversation. And the most important events which follow, the disclosure of the cross and the disclosure of the nails, are the results of the words of Judas (724-802) and of Elene (1074-1093). In its function of advancing the action of the story, direct discourse in the *Andreas* while not so important as in the *Juliana* is more important than in the *Elene*. Part of the situation at the beginning is revealed through the speeches of Matthew and God (59-117). And the beginning of the action proper, when God commands Andrew to journey to Mermedonia (167-224), the embarkation (254-351), and the journey itself (352-821) are developed for the most part by direct discourse. The means of entry to the city are made manifest by the direct words of God (925-976). So the attacks of the devil (1170-1218; 1281-1301; 1315-1385), the crisis in Andrew's torture (1398-1454), the summoning of the flood (1495-1521), and the Mermedonians' recognition of the true God,—all the important steps in the movement of the plot are developed for the most part by the direct words of the characters of the poem. The *Christ* has little action, but where the poem becomes narrative, direct discourse has a prominent place. We should note specially the dramatic colloquy of Joseph and Mary (164-213), thrust into Part I, which is not narrative; the speeches of God (476-490) and of the angels (510-526; 558-585) in the narrative of the Ascension; and the speeches of God in pronouncing the final doom of mankind (1344-1361; 1379-1523). And we should keep in mind the fact that Part I is written as a direct address, a series of supplications and hymns of praise.

In this direct discourse in the *Juliana* and the *Elene* there is no informal, idiomatic talk. We have, however, an approach to informal conversation in the first in the words of Africanus to Juliana (144-146), of the voice from the clouds (284-286), of the devil (632-634), of Heliseus (166-174), and of Juliana (317-

318).[29]   The shortest speech in the *Elene* is that of Judas,

> 'ic þā stōwe ne can
> nē pæs wanges wiht   nē þā wīsan cann.'   (683-684)

in the passage that is the nearest approach to realistic conversation which we find.

But in the *Andreas* we find much more natural, realistic conversation than in the other poems. We find much that is as near an approach to idiomatic talk as the nature of Old English poetry permits. God's message to Andrew in Achaia, beginning,

> Þū scealt fēran   ond ferð lædan,
> sīðe gesēcan,   ðær sylfætan
> eard weardigað,   ēðel healdaþ
> morðorcræftum.   (174-177),

and Andrew's answer,

> Hū mæg ic, Dryhten mīn,   ofer dēop gelād
> fōre gefremman   on feorne weg
> swā hrædlīce,   heofona scyppend,
> wuldres waldend,   swā ðū worde becwist?   (190-193),

are simple and to the point, realistic, except for the parallelisms which are one of the distinguishing characteristics of the Old English manner. So also, the talk of Andrew and the sea captain (256-348) is simple and natural with the exception of the kennings and repetitions, especially the lines where the captain asks for passage money,—

> Wē ðē ēstlīce   mid ūs willað
> fērigan frēolīce   ofer fisces bæð
> efne tō þām lande   þær þē lust myneð
> tō gesēcanne   syððan gē ēowre
> gafulrædenne   āgifen habbað,
> sceattas gescrifene,   swā ēow scipweardas,
> āras ofer ȳðbord,   unnan willað.   (292-298),

and where he expresses his surprise that Andrew should set out on a journey without proper equipment,—

> Hū gewearð þē þæs,   wine lēofesta,
> ðæt ðū sæbeorgas   sēcan woldes,
> merestrēama gemet,   māðmum bedæled,
> ofer cald cleofu   cēoles nēosan?
> Nafast þē tō frōfre   on faroðstræte
> hlāfes wiste   nē hlūtterne
> drync tō dugoðe?   Is se drohtað strang
> þām þe lagolāde   lange cunnaþ.   (307-314)

---

[29] See also 347-350; 456-460.

Again, note the natural words of the captain when fear seizes
Andrew's followers,—

> Læt nū geferian   flotan ūserne,
> lid tō lande   ofer lagufæsten,
> ond þonne gebīdan   beornas þīne,
> āras on earde,   hwænne ðū eft cyme.   (397-400)

And the conversation of Andrew and the captain on board the
ship (355-554) up to the point where Andrew begins to recite
more formally the deeds of the Savior is far more natural than
the speeches of the *Juliana* or the *Elene*.

In the *Christ* also we have as near an approach to realistic
conversation as the nature of Old English poetry permits in the
dramatic colloquy of Joseph and Mary in Part I,—

(Mary)   Ealā Iōsēph mīn,   Iācōbes bearn,
            mǣg Dāuīdes   mǣran cyninges,
            nū þū frēode scealt   fæste gedǣlan,
            ālǣtan lufan mīne!

(Joseph)   Ic lungre eam
            dēope gedrēfed,   dōme berēafod,
            forðon ic worn for þē   word[a] hæbbe
            sīdra sorga   ond sārcwida
            hearmes gehȳred,   ond mē hosp sprecað,
            tornworda fela. .   .   .   .
     .   .   .   .

(Mary)   Hwæt bemurnest ðū,
            cleopast cearigende? .   .   .
     .   .   .   .   .   .

(Joseph)   Ic tō fela hæbbe
            þæs byrdscypes   bealwa onfongen.
    .   .   .   .   (164-195)

This, with the speech of Mary which follows,—

> Sōð ic secge   þurh Sunu Meotudes,
> gǣsta Gēocend,   þæt ic gēn ne conn
> þurh gemæcscipe   monnes ōwer
> ǣnges on eorðon. .   .   .   .
> .   .   .   .   (197-213)

is the only instance of dialogue in the poem, unless we regard as
such as ll. 71-103, in which it is probable that the author wrote:

> Ealā wīfa wynn   geond wuldres þrym,
> .   .   .   .
> .   .   .   .   Swā eal manna bearn
> sorgum sāwað,   swā eft rīpað,—
> cennað tō cwealme.   (71-87)

as the words of the folk of Jerusalem, to which Mary replies in
ll. 89-103.

Dialogue in the *Juliana* is primarily only the formal colloquy. We have only one case where there are three speakers. When the devil tempts Juliana (ll.247-257) and claims to be God's angel (261-267), Juliana calls upon Heaven for the truth (272-282) and the voice of God answers her (284-286), but takes no further part in the conversation. And we have one case where the words of a third speaker are implied but not reported, when Heliseus sends orders for the maid to appear before the judgment seat (530-534) as she is in conversation with the devil. Juliana refuses, publicly, before the folk, to marry Heliseus (44-57); then Heliseus speaks with the father (68-88); then the father speaks with the daughter (92-157); and then Heliseus speaks with Juliana (166 ff). In no case do the father, the daughter, and the prince converse together. In no case have we the words of the folk who are witnessing the action.

These colloquies, although they are formal, are often dramatic in tone. In the meeting of Heliseus and the father of Juliana we have a critical situation portrayed with dramatic intensity in the words of the characters.

> "Mē þīn dohtor hafað
> geȳwed orwyrðu;   hēo mē on ān sagað,
> þæt hēo mǣglufan   mīnre ne gȳme,
> frēondrǣdenne.   .   .   .   .
>
> .   .   .   .
> "Ic þæt geswerge   þurh sōð godu,
> swā ic āre æt him   ǣfre finde
> oþþe, þēoden, æt þē   þīne hyldu
> winburgum in,   gif þās word sind sōþ,
> monna lēofast,   þe þū mē sagast,
> þæt is hȳ ne sparige,   ac on spild giefe,
> þeoden mǣra,   þē tō geweald[e]!
> Dēm þū hī tō dēaþe,   gif þē gedafen þince,
> swā tō līfe lǣt.   swā þē lēofre sȳ!"   (68-88)

We have the same kind of intense critical situation in the scene which concludes when the father hands over the daughter to the tortures of Heliseus (92-157), in the scene in which Heliseus attempts to win Juliana first by promises, then by threats (166-225), and in the scene in which the devil disguised as an angel is conquered by the maid (247-286).

Then we have the dramatic monologue in the speech of Juliana to Heliseus when she first refuses to marry him (ll. 46-

56), short, to the point; and in the two speeches of the devil as Juliana is being led to the place of execution (ll. 619-627; 632-634), again short and to the point. The only instance in the poem proper of the more formal, didactic, exhortatory sermon common to the Elene is the speech of Juliana just before her death (ll. 641-669). But the effect of the dramatic speeches in this poem is counteracted by the tedious digression of over 250 lines (289-553) in which the devil discourses to Juliana of his endless deeds of crime. This is in effect a monologue, an exposition of the nature and the deeds of the devil; for, although Juliana speaks four times during the recital, her words in each case amount to little more than 'say on.' The devil's speech is an exposition of his nature and his deeds in five parts:

1st. The recital of his crimes against Christ and the early Christians. 298-315

2nd. An account of his temptations in general. 321-344

3rd. An account of his methods of temptation. 352-415

4th. The devil's wonder at the strength of Juliana. 430-453

5th. A recital of further deeds of crime from the time of Adam on. 461-530

The dialogue in the *Elene* is always the formal colloquy. In no case are there more than two speakers. The assembled Jews speak as one man. It is true that the messengers of Elene come upon the Jews and break into their talk with Judas (550), but these messengers merely summon the men to the assembly and their words are not a part of the preceding argument. In the discussion which follows the discourse of Judas the author makes no attempt to report the words of many speakers. He describes the general conversation,

> Weoxan word cwidum: weras þeahtedon
> on healfa gehwæne sume hyder sume þyder,
> þrydedon ond þōhton. (547-549)

When Elene addresses the five hundred Jews (386-395), they answer with one accord,

> 'hwæt, wē ebrēisce æ leornedon,
> þā on fyrndagum fæderas cūðon,
> .   .   .   .
> .   .   .   . Wē ðæt æbylgð nyton,
> þe wē gefremedon on þysse folcscere,
> þēoden bealwa wið þec æfre.' (397-403)

Judas discourses at length on a matter of life and death (419-535) without interruption, although the highest excitement must have possessed his audience. And the wise men of the crowd answer with one accord, when Judas concludes, in the formal speech,

> 'næfre wē hȳrdon   hæleð ænigne
> on þysse þēode,   būtan þec nūðā,
> þegn ōðerne,   þyslic cȳðan
> ymb swā dȳgle wyrd.   .   .   .
>
> .   .   .   .   (538-546)

We find the set, formal colloquy also in the speech of Elene and the reply of the Jews (574-597) and in the discourses of Judas and the devil (903-953).

These colloquies are too expository or argumentative to be very dramatic in tone. The nearest approach to the mode of the drama is the series of colloquies of Judas and Elene (605-690). Here we have a touch of the tension that is characteristic of the drama, a spirit which clothes the words with the warmth of life. Such speeches as

> 'þē synt tū gearu,
> swā līf, swā dēað,   swā þē lēofre bið
> tō gecēosanne.   Cȳð ricene nū,
> hwæt ðū þæs tō þinge   þafian wille'   (605-608),
>
> 'ic þā stōwe ne can
> nē þæs wanges wiht   nē þā wīsan cann.'   (683-684),

and

> 'ic þæt geswerige   þurh sunu meotodes,
> þone āhangnan god,   þæt ðū hungre scealt
> for cnēomāgum   cwylmed weorðan,
> būtan þū forlǣte   þā lēasunga
> ond mē sweotollīce   sōð gecȳðe.'   (686-690),

serve well to bring before us the dramatic situation in which Elene forces Judas to choose between life and death, between right and loyalty to his folk. But the passage is marred by the slower argumentative speeches, as

> 'hwæt, wē ðæt hȳrdon   þurh hālige bēc
> hæleðum cȳðan,   þæt āhangen wæs
> on Caluarie   cyninges frēobearn,
> godes gāstsunu.   .   .   .   .
>
> .   .   .   .   (670-682)

The typical form of direct discourse in the *Elene* is the rather long, formal monologue. We have this in the two speeches of

Elene to the Jews (288-319; 333-376), in the speech of Judas to the Jews (419-535), in the prayers of Judas (726-802; 808-827), in the speech of Elene to Judas (1074-1093), and in the speech of the wise man (1168-1196). The nature of these formal speeches may be seen from the following plan of Elene's discourse to the second assembly of the Jews,—

    I.   These are the words of wisdom.

    II.   Ye were taught that the Lord should be born in the likeness of a child.

        (*a*) Moses sang of this,

        (*b*) David sang of this, and

        (*c*) Isaiah sang of this.

    III. Ye were given wealth and power and were commanded to follow the Lord.

    IV. But ye have forsaken the true God.

And where we have dialogue, as in the discourses of Elene and the Jews and of Judas and the devil, the words of each individual seem to be not a spontaneous expression of thought and feeling, but a set speech.

Of the soliloquy we have no instance. The only direct discourse aside from what we have already noted is made up of the words of the angel to Constantine (79-85), the question of Constantine about the meaning of the cross (162-165), the brief speech of Elene to the Jews (406-410), the words of the messengers (551-554), the cry of Judas when he agrees to bring to light the cross (699-708), Elene's question about the crosses (853-859), and the words of praise of the multitude (1121-1125).

As we have seen, dialogue in the *Andreas* is not always the formal colloquy of the *Elene*. We have this formal colloquy in Matthew's supplication and the Lord's answer (63-117), in the discourses of Andrew and the captain on the sea (557-817), beginning,—

```
Saga, þances gléaw     þegn, gif ðú cunne,
hú ðæt gewurde        be werum twéonum,
þæt ðá árléasan        inwidþancum,
Iúdéa cynn        wið Godes bearne
áhóf hearmcwide.        (557-561),
```

in the speeches of God and Andrew after the arrival in Mermedonia . (920-976), in Andrew's argument with the devil

(1360-1385), and in Andrew's appeal to God and its answer
(1401-1445).

The *Andreas,* moreover, shows in the use of conversation more
variety than the *Juliana* or the *Elene,* for in four places more
than two speakers take part in the discourse. On board the ship
Andrew informs the captain that his men are sore afraid (386-
395); the captain answers that they may be put ashore (397-
400); and the men ask with one accord,—

> Hwider hweorfað wē   hlāfordlēase,
> gēomormōde,   gōde orfeorme,
> synnum wunde,   gif wē swīcað þē?   (405-407)

After the arrival in Mermedonia, Andrew informs his men that
the captain of the ship was God himself (851-856); then the men
describe their vision of Heaven (859-891); Andrew calls upon
the Lord (897-909); and the Lord answers him (914-916).
Again, after God rescues the youth who is about to be sacrificed,
the Mermedonians express their need for the counsels of wise
men (1165-1167); the Devil advises them to seek out Andrew
and put him to death (1173--1183); and Andrew reviles the devil
(1185-1194). And when the thanes of hell fail in their attack
upon Andrew, the devil asks,

> Hwæt wearð ēow swā rōfum,   rincas mīne,
> lindgesteallan,   þæt ēow swā lȳt gespēow?   (1343-1344);

one of the thanes tells of Andrew's power (1347-1359); the
devil boasts of his own might (1362-1374); and Andrew answers
that the word of God shall conquer the Prince of Hell (1376-
1385).

The colloquies of the *Andreas,* more natural and less formal
than those of the *Elene* and the *Juliana,* are also more dramatic.
There is present in the speeches of the *Andreas* more of the
tension or suspense as to the outcome that is characteristic of the
drama. Our interest is held by an emotional appeal more than
by an intellectual. Matthew and Andrew pray fervently to God,
when death stares them in the face; upon God's answer hinge
their fates. Andrew discourses with the captain concerning
passage on the ship; upon the captain's answer depends the
fulfillment of God's command to rescue Matthew. Andrew calls
upon God after his arrival in Mermedonia; upon God's aid

depends Andrew's entrance into the city. In fact, the only speech in the poem which has for its main purpose the exposition of God's power is the discourse on the sea, in which Andrew endeavors to explain to the captain the glory and the power of Christ.

In the *Andreas*, the rather long, formal monologue, typical of the *Elene*, has little place. Andrew's long account of Christ's miracle (644-817) resembles somewhat the devil's discourse to Juliana; but it surpasses the latter in that it is narrative rather than expository and in that it does not lose sight of the captain. We do not feel that it is an explanation that serves its own end. We feel that it is an answer to the question of the captain, that it is part of a colloquy rather than a monologue. Andrew's prayers to God (897-909; 1401-1428), his answers to the devil (1185-1194; 1376-1385), his address to the pillar (1498-1521), and some of the speeches of God (926-976; 1431-1445) are rather formal and didactic, but they are brief and they are incorporated as essential steps in the progress of the action. The address to the pillar will serve to illustrate this point. Andrew bids the rock send forth a flood upon the Mermedonians (1498-1508). Then he continues,—

> Hwæt! ðū golde eart,
> sincgife, sylla;   on ðē sylf cyning
> wrāt, wuldres God,   wordum cyðde
> recene gerȳno,   ond ryhte ǣ
> getācnode   on tȳn wordum,
> Meotud mihtum swið;   Moyse sealde,
> swā hit soðfæste   syðþan hēoldon,
> mōdige magoþegnas,   māgas sīne
> godfyrhte guman,   Iosua ond Tobias,   (1508-1516),

probably with the conscious purpose of calling to the minds of his audience the importance of the ten commandments and the glory of Moses, Joshua, and Tobias; yet this purpose is not thrust upon us, for the speech is the natural one for the man in the position of Andrew.

Finally, we have seen that the only instances of conversation in the *Christ* are dramatic in form. One of them is so positively dramatic as to lead some to think that characters representing Joseph and Mary spoke the words of the dialogue before the eyes of the audience.

The rather long, formal monologue, common in the *Elene*, is not found in the *Christ*. The nearest approach to it is the speech of God to the evil ones on the Day of Doom (1379-1514; 1519-1523). But this is not coldly didactic. It is full of passion. It is not a lesson thrust into the narrative, but a heightened expression of the strongest emotion. Its outline is as follows:

I. I created thee and honored thee above all the earth, yet thou didst break my commandment and wast doomed to Hell.

II. I took upon myself the form of man in order to save thee, yet thou didst inflict upon me the direst torments.

III. Thou didst forsake the life which I bought for thee with my blood.

IV. I was poor that thou mightest be rich, yet thou wast not grateful.

V. Ill hast thou performed my command to cherish my brethren. Hence thou shalt suffer torments forever.

VI. Depart, thou accursed one, into eternal fires.

Then, we have the shorter speeches of God to the virtuous ones at the Judgment (1344-1361) and of Christ and of the angels at the Ascension (476-490; 510-526; 558-585). But in none of them do we find the didactic purpose predominant.

We have in direct discourse one supplication for deliverance through Christ (149-163) and one song of praise (403-415).

Lastly, we have quoted the direct words of God's command at the creation (230-232), of God's curse upon mankind (621-626), of the prophecy attributed to Isaiah (317-325), of the prophet (651-653), and of Solomon (715-719).

We should mention here that the actions of the narrative poems have much variety aside from what we have termed their methods of development. The *Juliana* introduces, as the plot progresses, no new characters except the devil and an angel, and the scene of the action is about the same throughout. But there is much variety in the torments inflicted upon the heroine and in the combination of natural and supernatural actions and characters.

More varied is the *Elene*. It has more characters of greater variety. Aside from the devil, it presents men and women, Roman and Hebrew. The scene of action is laid in the land of the Romans, on the sea, in the land of the Greeks, and in the land of the Jews. There are battles, sea voyages, land journeys, councils, punishments, miracles, and the final conversion of the Jews.

And most varied is the *Andreas.* New characters, natural and supernatural, are introduced as the plot progresses. The scene is laid in Mermedonia, in Achaia, and on the sea. There are the tortures of Matthew, the miracle of God's promise of aid, the sea voyage with storm and calm, the miracle of the journey through the air, the wonderful entry into the city with the miracle of the death of the guards, the marvelous release of Matthew, the miracle of the melting swords, the many tortures of Andrew, the miraculous healing, the miracle of the flood, and the final conversion.

COMPARISON WITH THE BEOWULF AND WITH THE LATIN.

Thus we find that the methods of development in the *Juliana,* the *Elene,* the *Andreas,* and the *Christ,* are, aside from direct discourse, simple, objective narrative, with rare instances of indirect discourse, subjective narrative, description, exposition or comment on the action, general narration and general description, and lyric outbursts of praise, exhortation and supplication.

Now, when we compare the methods of plot development in the Christian epics with those in the *Beowulf,* we find that the latter contains simple, objective narrative,[30] including indirect discourse,[31] subjective narrative,[32] description,[33] exposition or comment on the action,[34] general narration[35] and general description.[36] In its use of these the *Beowulf* shows no marked dis-

---

[30] Lines 194-236; 710-836; 1492-1590; 2667-2723; etc.

[31] Lines 92-98; 199-201.

[32] Lines 49-50; 129-134; 170-171; 189-193; 232-233; 607-610; 669-670; 691-696; 753-757; 841-846; 1306-1309; 1529-1530; 1873-1880; 1905-1910; etc.

[33] Lines 301-311; 320-323; 994-996; 1408-1432; 1570-1573; etc.

[34] Lines 20-25; 1057-1062; 2764-2766; 3174-3177; etc. We shall note the significance of comment on the action under Plot Movement.

[35] Lines 4-11.

[36] Lines 1925-1962.

tinctions from the Christian epics either from the point of view
of narrative development or of inner history.

Here it is important to note that the Christian poems, particularly the *Christ*, differ from the *Beowulf* in that they increase
the lyric element and the sermon element. The note of personal
emotion which we have indicated in the *Christ*, is also found in
the *Juliana*,—

> N[ū] ic þec, beorna Hlēo,   biddan wille,
> ēce, ælmihtig,   þurh þæt æþele gesceap,
> þe þū, Fæder engla,   æt fruman settest,
> þæt þū mē ne lǣte   of lofe hweorfan
> þīnre ēadgife.   (272-276),

in the *Elene*,—

> hālig is se hālga   hēahengla god,
> weoroda wealdend.   Is ðæs wuldres ful
> heofun ond eorðe   ond eall hēahmægen
> tīre getācnod.   (751-754),

and in the *Andreas*,—

> Sīe ðē ðanc ond lof,   þeoda waldend,
> tō wīdan fēore   wuldor on heofonum,
> ðæs ðū mē on sāre,   sigedryhten mīn,
> ellþēodigne,   ān ne forlǣte.   (1451-1454)

This indicates a somewhat advanced stage of narrative development, and a method of composition far from that of the scop,
far from what we term popular.

The lyric element of the Christian poems, as we have already
noted, may be due to the influence of the emotional Latin prose
and to the Latin hymns of the early church. But we must not
lose sight of the fact that the *Beowulf* has the beginnings of the
personal note in such passages as,—

> Hȳ bēnan synt,
> þæt hīe, þēoden mīn,   wið þē mōton
> wordum wrixlan;   nō ðū him wearne getēoh
> ðīnra gegn-cwida,   glædman Hrōðgār.   (364-367)

and

> Ðisse ansȳne   Al-wealdan þanc
> lungre gelimpe.   Fela ic lāþes gebād,
> grynna æt Grendle;   ā mæg God wyrcan
> wunder æfter wundre,   wuldres Hyrde.   (928-931)

This and the lyric quality of the *Seafarer*, the *Wanderer*, the

Ruined City, Deor's Lament, the *Love Letter,*[37] and the *Banished Wife's Complaint* make it at least possible that the lyric element in the religious epics is again a natural development within the field of Old English literature, merely emphasized or confirmed by the influence of the Latin.

Again, the element of sermonizing, or the emotional exposition, of the Christian epics shows a stage of development farther from primitive popular poetry than is the stage represented by the *Beowulf*. This element, aside from the *Christ*, is found in the *Juliana* in the discourse of the devil (289-530) and in the final speech of the heroine (641-669) ; in the *Elene,* in the speeches of Elene (288-319; 333-376) and of Judas (726-802) ; and in the *Andreas* in the discourse on the sea (537-817) and in the address to the pillar (1498-1521).[38] For the origin of the sermonizing element we may look to the Latin homilies of the early church or to the Old English sermons of the time. But here again we may state that no Latin influence was necessary. The change of heart occasioned by Christianity in itself accounts for the sermon element in the Christian epics. We may regard the influence of the Latin merely as a confirming one. And this view becomes stronger when we recall that emotional exposition of this kind is not unknown in the *Beowulf.* The speech of Hrothgar (1758-1781) is a natural forerunner of the emotional exposition of the other poems.

Then, in taking up more particularly the most important of all methods of development in the Christian epics, direct discourse, we have found that while dialogue is generally the formal colloquy, there are cases where there is an approach to natural conversation, and, particularly in the *Andreas,* where there are more than two speakers. We have found that the dramatic element becomes more and more important in the dialogue until we have in the *Christ* the distinct form of the drama. Then, we have found that a very important form of direct discourse is the monologue, either dramatic or formal and didactic. And finally, we have found that direct discourse, particularly in the *Christ,* is used in quotations for authority.

[37] Formerly designated *Riddle 61* and the *Husband's Message.*

[38] Krapp indicates passages of the *Andreas* which are evident reminiscences of the homiletic style.—*Andreas and the Fates of the Apostles,* pp. 92, 157.

In the *Beowulf,* too, direct discourse is the most important
of all methods of development. To it are given up two-fifths of
the poem. Here dialogue is always the formal colloquy. In no
case are there more than two speakers. Wulfgar announces to
Hrothgar the coming of Beowulf (361-370), Hrothgar orders
him to bid Beowulf to enter (372-389), and Wulfgar goes out
and delivers the message (391-398). The three do not join in
conversation. So after Hrothgar's reply (457-490) to Beowulf's
greeting (407-455), Unferth taunts Beowulf (506-528), but there
is a distinct break between the last two speeches. The three men
do not speak in a common conversation. We have the formal
colloquy in the speeches of the coast guard and Beowulf (237-
319), of Wulfgar and Beowulf (333-355; 391-398), of Wulfgar
and Hrothgar (361-389), of Beowulf and Hrothgar (407-490;
928-979; 1322-1396; 1818-1865), of Beowulf and Unferth (506-
607), and of Beowulf and Higelac (1987-2162).

The nature of these formal colloquies is well illustrated by
the speech of Beowulf, when he first meets Hrothgar,—

```
Wæs þū, Hrōðgār, hāl!     Ic eom Higelāces
mǣg ond mago-ðegn;       hæbbe ic mǣrða fela
ongunnen on geogoþe.     Mē wearð Grendles þing
on mīnre ēþel-tyrf       undyrne cūð;
secgað sǣ-līðend         þæt þes sele stande,
reced sēlesta,           rinca gehwylcum
īdel ond unnyt,          siþðan ǣfen-lēoht
under heofenes hador     beholen weorþeð.
      .    .    .    .    .    .    .    .    .
      .    .    .    .    .    .    .    .    .
Onsend Higelāce,         gif mec hild nime,
beadu-scrūda betst,      þæt mīne brēost wereð,
hrægla sēlest;           þæt is Hrēðlan lāf,
Wēlandes geweorc.        Gǣð ā wyrd swā hīo scel.     (407-455)
```

and by Hrothgar's reply,—

```
F[or w]ere-fyhtum þū,     wine mīn Bēowulf,
ond for ār-stafum         ūsic sōhtest.
Geslōh þīn fæder          fǣhðe mǣste,
wearþ hē Heaþolāfe        tō hand-bonan
mid Wilfingum;            ðā hine Wedera cyn
for here-brōgan           habban ne mihte.
      .    .    .    .    .    .    .    .    .
      .    .    .    .    .    .    .    .    .
```

Ðonne wæs þēos medo-heal   on morgen tīd
driht-sele drēor-fāh,   þonne dæg līxte,
eal benc-þelu   blōde bestȳmed,
heall heoru-drēore;   āhte ic holdra þȳ lǣs,
dēorre duguðe,   þē þā dēað fornam.
Site nū tō symle   ond onsǣl meoto,
sige-hreð secgum,   swā þīn sefa hwette.   (457-490)

We have also the formal monologue.[39] One of the speeches of Wealhtheow will serve to illustrate this,—

Brūc ðisses bēages,   Bēowulf lēofa,
hyse, mid hǣle,   ond þisses hrægles nēot,
þēo[d]-gestrēona,   ond geþēoh tela;
cen þec mid cræfte,   ond þyssum cnyhtum wes
lāra līðe;   ic þē þæs lēan geman.
Hafast þū gefēred   þæt ðē feor ond nēah
ealne wīde-ferhþ   weras ehtigað,
efne swā sīde   swā sǣ bebūgeð
windge [e]ard-weallas.   Wes, þenden þū lifige,
æþeling ēadig;   ic þē an tela
sinc-gestrēona.   Bēo þū suna mīnum
dǣdum gedēfe,   drēam healdende.
Hēr is ǣghywlc eorl   ōþrum getrȳwe,
mōdes milde,   man-drihtne hol[d];
þegnas syndon geþwǣre,   þēod eal gearo.
Druncne dryht-guman,   dōð swā ic bidde.   (1216-1231)

In both the colloquy and the monologue we have formal speeches. In each case they seem to be of the occasional nature Beowulf's speech of greeting to Hrothgar strikes us as a thing carefully prepared for the occasion. So with Hrothgar's reply. And Wealhtheow's words form a typical speech of a queen on the occasion of presenting a gift in gratitude for the delivery from the power of a monster. Even the shorter speeches, as that of the guard,—

Mǣl is mē tō fēran;   Fæder al-walda
mid ār-stafum   ēowic gehealde
sīða gesunde!   Ic tō sǣ wille
wið wrāð werod   wearde healdan.   (316-319)

and those of Beowulf in ll. 342-347; 2155-2162; 2511-2515; 2813-2816 never approach natural, realistic conversation.

---

[39] Lines 632-638; 655-661; 677-687; 1169-1187; 1216-1231; 1474-1491; 1652-1676; 1700-1784; 2426-2509; 2511-2515; 2518-2537; 2633-2660; 2663-2668; 2729-2751; 2794-2808; 2813-2816; 2864-2891; 2900-3027; 3077-3109; 3114-3119.

The fact that the dialogue of the Christian epics which we are studying is less formal and more realistic, particularly in including more than two speakers, and the fact that the monologue is less occasional and more natural mark a distinct advance upon the *Beowulf*. Again, there is a distinct advance in the Christian epics because the dramatic element is stronger. The speeches of the *Beowulf* are rhetorical, but they are not dramatic. When the coast guard asks Beowulf's business (237-257), we feel that he is going through the formal mode of questioning a stranger. When Beowulf announces his purpose to Hrothgar (407-455), we feel that he is formally asking to do what can not possibly be denied him. And so, throughout the poem, the dialogue lacks the stress of the drama. There is nothing to compare with the situation in the *Elene* (604-708), where the heroine endeavors to force Judas to disclose the hiding place of the cross. We have already pointed out that the Old English Christian poems probably derived something of their dramatic elements from the Latin. But we must not forget that the *Beowulf* has the beginnings of dramatic dialogue in such speeches as those of Hrothgar and Beowulf in ll. 1321-1396, where Beowulf offers his services to avenge the death of Æschere. And we must not forget that the *Seafarer* is dramatic in form and that the dramatic monologue is found in the *Banished Wife's Complaint*, *Deor's Lament*, the *Wanderer*, and the *First Riddle*.

In the *Beowulf* also, direct discourse which does not further the main action is employed in practically all of the functions which we found in the other poems.

The great difference between the *Beowulf* and the Christian epics is that, while in the latter direct discourse is an important factor in advancing the main action, in the former it is very unimportant. It is true that direct discourse which advances the action is found in the *Beowulf*, as in the speeches where Beowulf gains Hrothgar's permission to fight against Grendel (407-490), where Beowulf promises to slay Grendel's mother (1384-1396), and where Wiglaf goes to the rescue of the hero (2633-2668). But even in these cases the action is advanced but very slowly by the words of the characters. Wiglaf sees his lord hard pressed in battle with the dragon (2605), he draws his sword (2610), and finally delivers a formal speech of twenty-eight lines, recalling the old promises of the men to stand by their lord, before going to Beowulf's aid. The most important steps in the action of the poem, the fight with Grendel, the fight with Grendel's mother, and the fight with the dragon are not developed by direct discourse.

In general, direct discourse in the *Beowulf* retards the action instead of advancing it. To make this manifest it is only necessary to recall that after the fight with Grendel we have Hrothgar's speech of thanks (928-956), Beowulf's account of the fight (958-979), the song of the scop (1068-1159), and two speeches of Wealhtheow (1169-1187; 1216-1231), one hundred and seventy-eight lines of direct discourse which does not advance the action, before we come to Grendel's mother. After the fight with Grendel's mother we have two hundred and twenty-seven lines of direct discourse before we come to the dragon.

This tendency of the *Beowulf* to employ direct discourse only in those parts of the poem in which there is no progress in the action shows a stage of narrative growth not so far advanced as that of the Christian epics. It denotes, or at least suggests, a method of composition nearer to that of the scop, who would be prone to delay in finding his way from one main incident to another.

VI.

PLOT MOVEMENT.

We have seen that the plots of the Cynewulfian poems are developed with much variety of action. Now, when we come to examine the movement of the plot, the progress from beginning to end, we may say first that the action of the *Juliana,* if we omit the digressive discourse of the devil (289-530), is not only varied but simple and swift.

The movement of the plot of the *Juliana* is simple. The actions succeed each other chronologically in a single line. There are no synchronous actions unless we regard as such the destruction of Heliseus and the bearing of the body of Juliana to the city (671-695). Here probably the author intended one to follow the other in the order given. When Juliana engages the devil in the long recital of his crimes (289-530), we are given no notice of the doings of Heliseus. Juliana dismisses the devil, when she is summoned to appear before the judgment seat (530-558) ; but the devil's actions are not noted up to the time when he appears again to reproach Juliana (614).

While we have no complication of action, no treatment of synchronous events, in the *Juliana,* we have what approaches it when the story drops one character for the time being and forces us to hold in mind the earlier situation while we are on a new line of action. Thus Heliseus is not heard of while Juliana is engaged with the devil, yet the story has not done with him. We must hold him in mind until the time when his messengers arrive to summon Juliana (530).

Moreover, the action of the *Juliana,* aside from the digression, is swift. To make this clear we need only to recall that the author introduces the characters (1-41), develops his story through eleven distinct actions,—Juliana's refusal to marry Heliseus, the meeting of Heliseus and Africanus, the meeting of the father and the daughter, Heliseus' offer of pardon, the scourging of Juliana, the scourging and hanging by the hair, the capture of the devil, the attempted burning, the attempted

boiling in molten lead, the death of Juliana, the death of
Heliseus (41-288; 530-688),—and adds a conclusion (688-695)
in the space of 453 lines. But the effect of the swift action of
the plot proper is lost through the delay in the progress of the
story common to Old English poetry.

In the *Elene* the movement of plot is again simple. The
actions of the story succeed each other in chronological order
without overlapping. We have the description of the barbarian
hosts marching upon Rome (18-41) and then the preparations
of the Romans (41-65), not while the barbarians are marching
but after they have pitched camp. We have no hint of Elene's
action while Judas is haranguing the Jews (417 ff) or while her
messengers go to Rome and return (980 ff). But we have here
again the approach to synchronous actions when we must hold in
mind the position of the heroine during the time in which the
story centers about Judas and the Jews (417 ff). She is present
to our minds during this time although she does not reappear
in the action until she summons the fourth assembly (549 ff).

Again, if we omit the long, digressive discourse of Judas
(417-546), the action of the *Elene*, while not so swift as that of
the *Juliana*, is by no means slow. The spirited introduction
takes us through the conversion of Constantine as a result of his
victory in battle with the cross as his emblem (1-193). Then we
have briefly the journey of Elene and the four councils of the
Jews (194-416; 547-597), the incident in which Elene overcomes
Judas, the discovery of the crosses, and the miracle by which
the true cross is distinguished (598-894), the war of words
between Judas and the devil (895-967), the embassy to Constantine, the building of the temple, the conversion of Judas, the
finding of the nails, the disposal of the nails (968-1201), and
the conclusion (1202-1236).

When we consider that all of this material is developed in
1106 lines, the story does not appear to be at all drawn out. But
the movement seems to be much slower than in the *Juliana*,
because the first three councils of the Jews lack action. Elene
preaches to them (286-319; 332-376; 384-395), but nothing
happens. The long prayer of Judas (724-802) seems to aim to
turn us to Christ instead of to advance the action of the story.

And the discussion between Judas and the devil (895-967) is an unnecessary delay.

As in the *Juliana* and the *Elene,* the movement of plot in the *Andreas* is simple. The events of the story are presented without complication in chronological order. The introduction informs us that Matthew is awaiting death in the Mermedonian prison (1-167). God summons Andrew to the rescue; and the story is concerned with the doings of Andrew from line 167 to line 1003. We hear nothing of Matthew until Andrew arrives at the Mermedonian prison. But we have here the approach to synchronous actions which we noted in the *Juliana* and the *Elene.* We hold Matthew in mind during the journey of Andrew. We know of the actions of Matthew although the story does not note them.

So, too, the plot movement of the *Andreas,* like that of the *Juliana,* is swift, if we omit the long discourse on the sea (469-821). The introduction informs us clearly of the position of Matthew (1-167). Then follow the journey of Andrew on the sea and through the air, the destruction of the guards, and the release of Matthew (167-467; 822-1057). Now we have the assembly of the Mermedonians, the selection of one of their number to be sacrificed as food for the rest, and the miracle of the melting swords (1058-1154). Then follow the series of tortures inflicted upon Andrew and his final healing (1155-1477), the destructive flood, the withdrawal of the waters, the miracle of the restoration of the Mermedonians to life, and the conversion of the Mermedonians to Christianity (1492-1722). The fact that all of these varied actions are developed in the space of 1352 lines is sufficient evidence to show the swiftness of the plot movement of the *Andreas.* But again there are delays.

Delays of plot movement in Old English poetry in general are of four kinds,—comments on the action, digressions, episodes, and repetitions. For convenience I have used the term digressions to denote accounts of the characters in the stories or of things and events with which those characters are immediately concerned. I have used the term episodes to denote stories retold in a poem for their own interest. The account of the swimming match in the *Beowulf* is a digression, while the account of Finn and Hnaef is an episode. *See summary*

Of the first of these four kinds of delays, brief comments of
the author on the action, the *Juliana* has no instance. The *Elene*
has six instances,—ll. 210-211; 837-839; 893-894; 896; 1027-1033;
1229-1236. And the *Andreas* has four,—ll. 120-121; 979-980;
1150-1154; 1478-1491.

The second kind of delay, the digression, we have in the
Juliana in the words of the devil (429-453). This speech is
apart from the main action of the story, yet it serves to emphasize
the power which God has bestowed upon the heroine. It interests
us for its bearing upon Juliana as one of the characters of the
plot proper. So, too, the general account of the deeds of the
devil (289-428; 454-530), while it partakes somewhat of the
character of the episode, bears upon the nature of the devil who
tempts the maid and upon the nature of the maid who can
resist such temptation. Digression seems at first thought to be
abundant in the *Elene*. We are apt to regard the speeches of
the heroine to the Jews (286-319; 332-376) and the prayer of
Judas (724-802) as digressions, but we should not do so. While
these speeches are concerned with the treatment of Christ by
the Jews and with the nature and power of God, material appar-
ently aside from the events of the plot proper, they furnish, not
digressions from the main actions of the plot, but specific details
of those actions. The only instance of digression in the *Elene*
is that part of the speech of Judas which relates the experiences
of his father (436-527). This is what I have termed digression
rather than what I have termed episode, because it tells of the
Crucifixion, the martyrdom of Stephen, the Ascension, and the
conversion of Saul not for their own sake but for their influence
upon Judas. In the *Andreas* we have an instance of the digression in the first part of the conversation between Andrew and
the captain on the sea (471-554). Here we have not the episode
interesting for its own sake, but the digression which serves to
emphasize the marvelous skill of the captain, one of the personages of the story. Again we have a digression in the account of
the vision of Heaven (859-891), which serves to emphasize the
miracle of the transportation to Mermedonia and the attitude
of God toward Andrew. A third digression (1701-1705) tells
of the fate of Andrew,—not what happened to him in this story,

but his final end. Lastly, we might call Andrew's account of
how Christ stilled the sea (438-457) a digression. Yet, this is
very closely related to the main action of the plot. It serves to
quiet the fears of the men. It makes possible the miracle of the
transportation through the air.

The *Juliana* and the *Elene* contain no episodes. The *Andreas*
has only one. This is the second part of the discourse on the
sea (555-817), which is concerned with the doings of Christ and
his apostles not for their connection with the story but for their
intrinsic interest.

Of the fourth kind of delay, repetition, the *Juliana* has
nothing except the single case where we have the two parallel
statements,—

Swylt ealle fornōm
secga hlōþe   ond hine sylfne mid,
ǣr þon hȳ tō lande   geliden hæfdon,
þurh þearlīc þrēa.   (675-678)

and

Þær XXX wæs
ond fēowere ēac   fēores onsōhte
þurh wǣges wylm   wigena cynnes,
hēane mid hlāford;   hrōþra bidǣled
hyhta lēase   helle sōhton.   (678-682)

Here the repetition, which adds new details, seems to be due to
the inability of the author to express all the details of the picture
without retracing his steps. Of the episode the *Elene* contains
no instance, and it contains only two instances of repetition,—

Werod samnodan,
Hūna lēode   ond Hrēðgotan.   (19)
Lungre scynde
ofer burgenta   beaduþrēata mǣst
hergum tō hilde.   (30 ff)

and

Swylce Iūdas onfēng
æfter fyrstmearce   fulwihtes bæð.   (1033)
þā wæs gefulwad,   sē ðe ǣr feala tīda
lēoht gearu.   (1044)

In each case the second follows immediately after the first statement and in each case it adds new details. The *Andreas* is almost
free from repetition. In ll. 14-18,—

> þām hālig God   hlȳt getēode
> ūt on þæt īgland,   þǣr ǣnig þā gīt
> ellþēodigra   ēðles ne mihte
> blǣdes brūcan;   oft him bonena hand
> on herefelda   hearde gescēode,

we have the general statement of the character of the Mermedonians and of the fate of Matthew among them. This is the
summary introduction which leads up to the more particular
accounts of the Mermedonian land (19-39) and Matthew's experience therein (40-58). Here we do not have the repetition
of the account of an event of the story. Lines 14-18 contain
little more than a reference to what is stated in detail in lines
19-58. God's speech to Andrew (174-188) repeats briefly the
description of the Mermedonians and Matthew's position among
them,—

		Repetition of
They are cannibals holding their land in crime.	175-177	19-25.
They grant life to no stranger.	177-182	15-17;25-28.
Among them Matthew is fast in bonds.	183-184	48-50.
They are to kill him in three days.	185-188	147-154.

Again, the captain repeats to Andrew the fact that strangers
cannot dwell in Mermedonia (279-282), which summarizes what
has been given in 15-17; 25-28; 177-182. Here we have a very
natural repetition in the realistic speeches of the characters,
summary accounts of what has already been presented, with no
new details. The only other case of possible repetition in the
Andreas is ll. 941-943, where God says to Andrew,

> Wāt ic Māthēus   þurh mǣnra hand
> hrinen heorudolgum,   hēafodmāgan
> searonettum beseted,   (941-943)

which, like the preceding, is a perfectly natural reference to what
has gone before.

We can speak of plot movement only in certain sections of
the *Christ*, for in much of the poem there is no action. Part I
is not narrative. The succession of lyric outbursts supplemented
by expository comments, moreover, as we have seen, shows no
orderly progress of thought or feeling. In Part II the first
section (440-585) is the narration of Christ's ascension. If we
regard the speech beginning with line 558 as a continuation of

that which closes with line 526, this section shows a simple orderly narrative development. There is here no overlapping, no synchronous action. Part III has very little of what we may call plot movement, yet it has much of the action, characteristic of narrative, which stirs our interest in the outcome. This part of the poem may be termed narration developed by a series of descriptions. The series of pictures, as we have already noted, has a progressive movement, for each new one adds details which have not been included in the preceding ones. The movement is on a larger scale that which is known as incremental repetition in the ballads. One example will serve to make this clear. In the first picture (875-920) we have the sounding of trumpets which summons all mankind unto Mount Zion. Unto the assembly comes Christ in a blaze of glory, gentle toward His chosen ones but terrible toward the wicked. In the second picture (930-1026) we have again the coming of Christ. As He approaches fires sweep over the earth and the lights of Heaven fall headlong. The Lord visits all creation with consuming fires, and then comes to Mount Zion in great majesty. This repetition of the first picture with added details cannot be called a simple movement or progress; but it is not similar to the complication that would result from the descriptions of synchronous actions. We do have one marked instance of the treatment of synchronous actions in ll. 1234-1300, which explain first the three signs which appear unto the blessed and second the three signs which appear unto the doomed at the same time.

Thus the plot movement of the *Christ*, where we may speak of plot movement, is slow. The only exception is the first section of Part II, which has an orderly progress without delay from beginning to end.

Then, the didactic purpose of the *Christ*, much more prominent than in the other poems, causes the author to comment on the action and to draw lessons appropriate to the Advent season to a much greater extent than in the more purely narrative poems which we have been considering. We have in the *Christ* about fifty-five lines of brief comments by the author[1] and about three

---

[1] Lines 33-35; 219-223; 241-243; 468-470; 921-929; 1015-1021; 1056-1060; 1079-1080; 1081-1088; 1365-1369; 1598-1602; 1629-1633.

hundred and thirty lines of the longer expository accounts which do not differ from the shorter ones in nature.[2]

These expositions are not in any sense the same as what we have termed digressive accounts of the characters of the story or of the things or events with which those characters are concerned. The narrative portions of the *Christ* are delayed by comment, by exposition, but of digressions like those of the *Andreas* we have nothing. And of what we have termed the episode we have nothing.

Finally, we have already noted the delay in the movement of the *Christ* occasioned by repetition, the repetition that is due to the inability of the poet to present all the details that are present to his mind in one picture. Lines 930-1215 cover with new details the same ground as lines 867-874. And within the second of these groups we have again the same sort of repetition. Here there are four descriptions of the all-consuming fire (930-940; 941-971; 972-1006; 1039-1044) presented as if they were pictures of succeeding scenes.

COMPARISON WITH THE BEOWULF AND WITH THE LATIN..

The Plot of the *Beowulf*, too, has much variety in methods of development and in the actions themselves. And the movement of that plot is in general simple. Yet we have one instance of synchronous actions more marked than that of the *Christ*. When Beowulf is at the bottom of the mere, after the fight with the monster, he cuts off the head of Grendel (1590). Then the poet turns to those who are waiting for the hero on land (1591-1605); and with line 1605 he goes back to the action of Beowulf where he has left off at line 1590. This is the beginning of real complication in action. There are in the *Beowulf* also instances like those of the Christian epics where we have to hold in mind one character while the action is concerned with another, as in the account of the coming of Grendel's mother (1251-1299), where we hear nothing of Beowulf.

Then, the action of the *Beowulf* is not so swift as that of the *Juliana*, the *Elene*, or the *Andreas*. This is due to the great

---

[2] Lines 119-129; 135-146; 426-439; 600-620; 627-650; 654-714; 720-771; 779-796; 1090-1102; 1183-1215; 1301-1311; 1316-1333; 1549-1558; 1578-1590.

elaboration of those parts of the poem which lie between the main incidents. It is due to the greater number of the common delays which we have noted. To compare the *Beowulf* with the other poems in respect to these delays will be worth while for the light which such comparison will throw upon the topics of narrative development and "inner history," the genesis or manner of composition.

The *Beowulf* contains all four of the common kinds of delays in plot movement,—first, brief comments of the author on the action of the story; second, longer digressive accounts of the characters of the story or of things and events with which those characters are immediately concerned; third, episodes or stories retold in the poem for their own interest; and fourth, repetitions of the accounts of the actions of the story.

Of the first kind, brief comments of the author on the action of the story, we have in the *Beowulf* about forty-five lines.[3] These comments are of two kinds. The first is religious, Christian. For example, after the statement that the men of Heorot knew not the Lord, the author adds,—

> Wā biö þǣm ðe sceal
> þurh slīðne nīð   sāwle bescūfan
> in fȳres fæþm,   frōfre nè wēnan,
> wihte gewendan;   wel bið þǣm þe mōt
> æfter dēað-dæge   Drihten sēcean,
> ond tō Fæder fæþmum   freoðo wilnian.   (183-188)[4]

The second kind is not specifically Christian. In the description of Beowulf's fight with the mother of Grendel, after the words,—

> strenge getrūwode,
> mund-gripe mægenes,

the author adds,—

> Swā sceal man dōn,
> þonne hē æt gūðe   gegān þenceð
> longsumne lof,   nā ymb his līf cearað.   (1534-1536)[5]

---

[3] Lines 183-188; 700-702; 1002-1008; 1057-1062; 1534-1536; 1609-1611; 1691-1693; 2166-2169; 2291-2293; 2708-2709; 2764-2766; 2858-2859; 3056; 3062-3065; 3174-3177.

[4] See also ll. 700-702; 1057-1062; 1609-1611; 1691-1693; 2291-2293; 2858-2859; 3056.

[5] See also ll. 1002-1008; 2166-2169; 2708-2709; 2764-2766; 3062-3065; 3174-3177.

We should note here that the opportunity for specifically Christian comment in some cases seems to have been missed. In an original poem by a zealous Christian author we should not expect to find passages like the following,—

> Nō þæt ȳðe byð
> tō befleōnne,   fremme sē þe wille;
> ac gesacan sceal   sāwl-berendra,
> nȳde genȳdde,   niþða bearna,
> grund-būendra,   gearwe stōwe,
> þǣr his līc-homa   leger-bedde fæst
> swefeþ æfter symle.   (1002-1008),[6]

where the specifically Christian element does not appear.

Now, we find that in very early narrative forms, like the primitive ballads, the action is without comment. In the course of development the tendency is to add more and more comment on the action up to the stage where men begin to have theories of art, where men begin to study structure and technique. Thus, when we find that 0 per cent. of the *Juliana*, 1.2 per cent. of the *Andreas*, 23 per cent. of the *Christ*, and 1.4 per cent. of the *Beowulf* are made up of expository comment, we may infer that the *Beowulf* is more highly developed than the *Juliana*, the *Elene*, and the *Andreas*, and that the *Christ* is far more highly developed than the *Beowulf*. However, we must keep in mind the fact that since the *Christ* is not a narrative poem, little is to be gained by comparing it with the others. And we must remember that the more highly developed narrative form is not necessarily chronologically later than the less highly developed.

From the point of view of "inner history" we might conclude from our study of comments on the action either, first, that the genesis of the *Beowulf* was about the same as the genesis of the narrative poems of Cynewulf; that we may speak of an older pagan epic only as an indefinite source of material; or, second, that there existed an older pagan epic which was free from external comment; that the Christian who put the poem into the shape in which it has come down to us interpolated passages of expository comment; or, third, that there existed an older pagan epic which contained much of the scops' comment on the action; that the later Christian version of the story

---

6 See also ll. 3174-3177.

retained this characteristic of style; that the specifically Christian passages of the *Beowulf* are modifications of or additions to what was already there.

The first of these and the second seem to me less probable than the third. In the first case, even if we grant that the purpose of the *Beowulf* was primarily the edification of a future king or the rousing of the valor of a band of retainers, we must admit that a writer of the time of Cynewulf not influenced strongly by án earlier poem would have restricted himself more to purely Christian exposition. Or, in any case, he would not have missed the opportunity for Christian comment that lies in ll. 1002-1008; 3174-3177. In the second case, the writer who would add zealously Christian comments to an older pagan poem would probably add nothing else. His mind would be too much occupied with things specifically Christian to allow him to moralize about political marriages, etc.

So, the most probable view is the third. The presence of comment in a pagan poem which gradually became Christian, comment which was perhaps a traditional characteristic of the older epic, enjoyed by the public, led the final writer of the *Beowulf* to retain it as one of the natural parts of the story. He added to it, he modified it, we cannot say how much. But the nature of it is best explained by the supposition that it existed in the *Beowulf* as a marked characteristic before the story was Christianized.

Of the second main kind of delay, digressive accounts of the characters of the story or of the things or events with which they are immediately concerned, we have in the *Beowulf* five hundred and thirty-five lines,—the reference to an old account of the creation (90-98); Hrothgar's account of Beowulf's father (450-472); Unferth's taunt about the swimming match and Beowulf's account of it (499-606); the account of the Brosing necklace in comparison with the one presented to Beowulf (1197-1214); Hrothgar's advice to Beowulf (1709-1784); the contrast between Hygd and Thrytho (1921-1962); Beowulf's comment on the political marriage of Freawaru and Ingeld, the Heathobard (2024-2069); the account of Beowulf's exploits aside from those recorded in the plot proper (2354-2400); Beowulf's reminiscences

about Hrethel and Herebald, the strife between the Swedes and
the Geats, Hæthcyn's fall at Ravenswood, and the slaying of
Dæghrefn (2426-2509) ; and the messenger's account of the death
of Higelac, the fall of Hæthcyn, and the feuds of the Swedes and
the Geats (2913-3007).[7]

Here we have more than brief comments on the actions or
morals drawn from them. We have, moreover, not accounts which
are introduced merely because they are interesting in themselves.
We have the portrayal of a character strengthened by an account
of his actions which are not included in the main plot. In the
recital of the swimming match we see Beowulf in an adventure
which makes his triumph over Grendel more probable. The
account of Beowulf's father and that of his exploits, aside from
the killing of the dragon, after he has left the country of
Hrothgar, serve, too, to make the character of the man vivid.
Of the same class is the account of Hygd, who is made more
striking by comparison with Thrytho. Again we have the
description of the necklace presented to Beowulf made more vital
by comparison with the famous Brosing necklace, which otherwise
is of no interest to us. Finally we have accounts of and comments on events which, while not forming parts of the main
story, are closely related to it. Of this kind is Beowulf's comment on the marriage of Freawaru, who is interesting only
because she is the daughter of Hrothgar.

The fact that 33 per cent. of the *Juliana*, 6.9 per cent of the
Elene, 7 per cent. of the *Andreas*, and 16.7 per cent. of the
Beowulf are given up to digressions from the plots proper leads
us to conclude that the *Elene* and the *Andreas* show a marked
advance upon the *Beowulf* in narrative style, while the *Juliana*
shows a marked retrogression.[8]

From the point of view of inner history the large proportion
of digressions in the *Beowulf* in comparison with the *Elene* and

---

[7] Some of this material, particularly the account of the swimming match
and the account of Beowulf's exploits in ll. 2354-2400, is departure from
the chronological order rather than mere digression. But we are justified in
including such material under the term digression, as we have used it, since
the events recorded here do not affect us as parts of the main action.

[8] The proportion of the *Juliana* given up to digression might be somewhat different if we had the sixty-five to seventy-five lines which are lost
after l. 288 and the lines lost after l. 558.

the *Andreas* leads us to the conclusion that the first poem was probably developed by a series of scops who were influenced directly by a number of earlier poems containing many digressions, who in singing from memory were apt to wander from the main incidents of their stories. Men who wrote such poems as the *Andreas* and the *Elene* were far less apt to wander, since they had their stories as wholes well in hand before they began to write, since they were not influenced directly by earlier poems, and since they were not under the necessity of singing on without stop before the warriors in the hall.

And the large proportion of digressive material in the *Juliana* does not lead to the view that this poem had an inner history like that of the *Beowulf*. The *Juliana* was evidently composed in the same manner as the *Elene* and the *Andreas*. Its digression is not that of the scop who was apt to wander from the strict plot of his story. The poem contains not a number of digressions, but a single one. This strikes us not as the unconscious departure from the plot proper, but as the conscious retention of what was before the author in his Latin original. The author includes the long account of the wiles of the devil because, with his zeal for turning the hearts of his audience against that devil, he regards the digression as one of the most important parts of his work.

The writer of the *Beowulf*, too, had his story as a whole well in hand. But he had before him a story which had been developed by scops. Minstrels, depending upon memory and perhaps narrating spontaneously, knowing many stories about personages and events, naturally wandered from the straightforward path of the particular actions which held the main places in their songs. Digressions were unconscious. They became a characteristic mark of the older epics. The public became accustomed to them and liked them. The poet who gave the *Beowulf* its final form was familiar with the digressions of the popular epic developed by the minstrels. He liked them. He retained them.

Of the third kind of delay, the episodes or stories introduced into the poem for their own interest, the *Beowulf* has one hundred and thirty-three lines,—the scop's accounts of Sigemund, of Heremod, and of Finn and Hnæf (874-900; 901-915; 1068-1159). These episodes are accounts of characters or events which are not closely related to the characters or events of the main plot. The accounts of Sigemund, of Heremod, and of Finn and Hnæf have places in the poem merely because they were sung by the scop in the hall where the persons of the main story were assembled. It is true that episodes might serve to vivify the main plot by influencing the mood of the audience. It is quite conceivable, however, that they might be such as to induce a mood antagonistic to that which would render the main plot most effective.

From the point of view of narrative development, the fact that the *Juliana* and the *Elene* contain nothing of the episode, while the *Andreas* contains 15.2 per cent. and the *Beowulf* 4.1 per cent., leads us to conclude that the *Juliana* and the *Elene* show a distinct advance upon the *Beowulf* in narrative structure, while the *Andreas* shows a distinct retrogression. The retrogression in the *Andreas*, however, is not what the numbers seem to indicate. We must note that although the account of Christ's miracles in the *Andreas* does seem to be interesting for its own sake, yet it is more closely connected with the main plot than are the episodes of the *Beowulf*. The story of Finn and Hnæf has a place in the latter merely because the scop sings it. The scop might have sung any other song, which would have been included as is this one. The account of the miracles of Christ in the *Andreas* is the account of the deeds of one of the characters of the story, Christ, and of Andrew's association with the Lord. It serves to emphasize the power of Christ and the wisdom and the zeal of Andrew. In fact, it merges into what we have termed the digression.

From the point of view of ''inner history'' the episodes of the *Beowulf*, like the digressions, point to a manner of composition different from that of the *Elene*, the *Juliana*, and the *Andreas*. The episodes of the *Beowulf*, more positively than the digressions, confirm us in the view that the poem bears the mark of the influence of oral composition or of extemporaneous modification. The scop would not only digress from the main action of his narrative; he would even take up for a time a wholly distinct action. Again, the fact that the *Andreas* contains an episode of over two hundred lines does not weaken this view. We can see that the Christian author of the story of Andrew desired to express the story of Christ's miracles for its religious effect. Probably with the precedent of the heroic epic in mind, he inserted his account of Christ's miracles with much skill in the place best suited to it. In this case we see clearly the reason for the episode in the Christion zeal of the poet; in the *Beowulf* we see the reason for the episode in the influence of the oral compositions of the scops.

When we take up the fourth main kind of delay in plot movement, we note first that the *Beowulf* has repetitions of two of the main incidents of the story, the fight with Grendel and the fight with Grendel's mother. There are three distinct accounts of each of these incidents. The first account of the fight with Grendel is given in ll. 710-836, and the first account of the fight with Grendel's mother in ll. 1251-1625. The second account of each of these follows the action itself when Beowulf relates his adventures to Hrothgar. Lines 957-979 give us Beowulf's account of his fight with Grendel. This may be summarized as follows:

> I desired to kill Grendel outright so that his body should not escape. (963-966)
> I could not prevent his departure. (967-970)
> However, he had to leave his arm and shoulder behind. (970-977)

The facts of this account have already been given in ll. 758-761; 788-794; 815-818. It adds no new details, but it makes manifest Beowulf's modesty in his manner of reporting his own deeds. It comes into the story naturally in the speech of the hero.

So, too, Beowulf's account of his fight with Grendel's mother (1651-1670) is incorporated in the story naturally in the speech of the hero. It is summary. It adds no new details to the account which precedes it. After the general statement of the difficulty of the task, Beowulf tells of the failure of the good sword Hrunting, of the efficacy of the sword which he took from the wall, of the melting of the blade, and of the retention of the hilt. All of this has been presented with much more detail in ll. 1518-1528; 1557-1568; 1605-1611; 1612-1617. And here, as in the account of the fight with Grendel, the attitude of the hero toward his own deeds forms a new element of interest....

The third account of the killing of each of the monsters in the *Beowulf* is given in Beowulf's reply to Higelac's question as to the outcome of the adventures. In the following summary of

Beowulf's speech the numbers in the second column denote the lines which contain the facts which Beowulf repeats.

repetitions	*facts.*
The general statement that Hrothgar is avenged. 1999-2009	823-827; 1575-1584; 1669-1676
We went to greet Hrothgar. 2009-2010	320-488
Hrothgar assigned me a seat with his son. 2011-2013	489-494. (But the seat with the son is not mentioned till after the fight.)
There was joy in the hall. 2014-2016	497-498; 607-612; 642-643
The Queen passed among the men. 2016-2018	612-619
At times she bestowed a present. 2018-2019	620-622
Freawaru passed ale to the men. 2020-2024	
Freawaru is betrothed to Ingeld a Heathobard, for political reasons. 2024-2075	
Grendel came at night. 2069-2075	702-709
Hondscio was killed. 2076-2078	739-742 (Hondscio is not named.)
Grendel swallowed his body. 2078-2080	742-745
Grendel grappled with me. 2081-2085	745-753
A pouch was suspended over me. 2085-2088	
He desired to kill me with the others. 2089-2091	730-734
But he could not do so when I stood up in anger. 2091-2092	758-761
I gave him requital. 2093-2096	809-815
He retreated to his sea-cave bereft of his hand. 2096-2100	815-823; 970-979
Hrothgar rewarded me in the morning. 2101-2104	1020-1049
There was joy at the feast. Hrothgar questioned me. The minstrel sang. And the king mourned for the loss of his youthful strength. 2105-2117	991-996; 1011-1019; 1160-1165; 925-956; 1063-1160. (There is no particular case of mourning for youthful strength.)
At night Grendel's mother came for vengeance. 2117-2120	1276-1280
She killed Æschere 2120-2123 and carried away his body. 2124-2128	1294-1295; 1330-1344
The loss of Æschere was the worst of evils to Hrothgar. 2129-2130	1296-1300; 1306-1309; 1321-1329

Hrothgar asked me to display my prowess and promised rewards.	
2131-2134	1376-1382
I sought the monster in the mere.	
2135-2136	1399-1500
The contest was in doubt. 2137	1501-1556
The waters seethed with gore.	
2138	1591-1594
I cut off the monster's head with the sword. 2138-2140	1557-1590
I almost lost my life. 2140-2141	1541-1549
Hrothgar gave me presents.	
2142-2147	1866-1869

Here we have nowhere exact verbal repetition. There are variations of the first account as in 2011-2013 and in 2105-2117. There are additions of details, as in 2020-2024; 2024-2029; 2085-2088. There are omissions of details, as where Beowulf summarizes his first meeting with Hrothgar (2009-2010) in two lines when the first account (320-488) has nearly seventy lines. That is, we have the sort of modification that suggests conscious repetition with conscious changes for the sake of variety.

Aside from the three main accounts of the contests with Grendel and Grendel's mother, the *Beowulf* contains other repetitions of details connected with those contests. Hrothgar's attitude of hopelessness, the fact that he looked for no aid against Grendel, is made clear in ll. 144-174. This is repeated in his speech of thanks to Beowulf (929-942) and again in ll. 1769-1781. Again, Grendel's descent from Cain is brought out in ll. 102-114. This is repeated without any additional details in ll. 1263-1266. But here, or elsewhere, we do not find exact verbal repetition.

Then, the fact that Grendel is charmed against the sword, clearly stated in ll. 798-805, is repeated in ll. 987-990. But in the first case we have the description of the attempt to kill the monster by the sword, when the men knew not the charm,—

Hīe þæt ne wiston,—

while in the second case, the sight of the hand makes clear to all men that swords would have been useless.

When Beowulf comes upon the body of Grendel in the sea-cave, there is a brief account of that monster's offence against

Hrothgar in consuming thirty men (1578-1584). The manner
of the repetition here suggests that the audience has forgotten
much about Grendel or that the author is following an account
of Grendel's mother independent of that of Grendel.

In another case we have two accounts of the damage to
Heorot. The first occurs in ll. 770-775,—

> Reced hlynsode;
> þā wæs wundor micel,   þæt se wīn-sele
> wiðhæfde heaþo-dēorum,   þæt hē on hrūsan ne fēol,
> fæger fold-bold;   ac hē þæs fæste wæs
> innan ond ūtan   īren-bendum
> searo-þoncum besmiþod.

To this the second adds more specific details,—

> Wæs þæt beorhte bold   tōbrocen swīðe,
> eal inne-weard   īren-bendum fæst,
> heorras tōhlidene;   hrōf āna genæs
> ealles ansund.   (997-1002)

Finally, there are three brief summaries of the contest with
Grendel in ll. 1267-1276; 1333-1337; 2349-2354. These add no
new details. Yet, they are not mere references, such as we have
in Beowulf's words,

> Swā ic gīo wið Grendle dyde.   (2521)

The second of these comes in naturally in the speech of Hrothgar,
but the first and especially the third seem to refer to something
which is not a part of the matter in hand. Lines 2349-2354 refer
to the struggles with the monsters as if they were known to the
audience, yet not included in the poem. Beowulf did not fear
the dragon,

> forðon hē ǣr fela,
> nearo nēðende,   nīða gedīgde,
> hilde-hlemma,   syððan hē Hrōðgāres,
> sigor-ēadig secg,   sele fǣlsode,
> ond æt gūðe forgrāp   Grendeles mǣgum
> lāðan cynnes.

The *Beowulf* has also more than one account of the last great
event of the poem, the killing of the dragon. Immediately after
Beowulf's death follows a summary of the dragon's life and
death and a repetition of the end of the hero.

The coiled dragon no longer could
govern the treasure.   2826-2827   2777-2782[9]

Through the bite of the sword he
had fallen to earth near his hoard.
                                    2828-2831   2702-2708

No longer could he fly through the
air at midnight, gloating over his
treasure.   2832-2835

Few cared to face the fire-dragon
or to molest his hoard.   2836-2842   2409-2413; 2596-2601

Beowulf and the dragon met death.
                                    2842-2845   2772; 2819-2826

Again, Wiglaf repeats the victory of Beowulf without followers and the fact that the monster became weaker when he
(Wiglaf) did the little that he could (2873-2883), which have
already been brought out in ll. 2694-2708.

Then the messenger repeats the result of the contest with the
dragon and some of its details,—

Beowulf and the dragon are dead.
                                    2900-2904   2772; 2819-2826

The sword was useless.
                                    2904-2906   2583-2586

Wiglaf sits over Beowulf.
                                    2906-2910   2852-2854

Wiglaf tells of the hard fate that
they met.   3084-3086   2709-2711

Of bearing out the treasure to his
lord.   3087-3093   2752-2792

And of Beowulf's orders for his
funeral.   3093-3100   2792-2808

And finally we have repetition in the description of the dead
dragon,

The fire-spewing monster was
scorched by the flames.   3038-3041

He was fifty feet long.   3042-3043

He came forth at night and re-
turned to his den.   3043-3045   2302-2320

Death was fast upon him.
                               3045-3046   2702-2708; 2772; 2824-2835

Here, in nearly every case the repetitions are introduced
naturally in the speeches of the characters. And they add new
details. They may be due to a certain extent to the inability of
the author to include all of the details of the scene in one picture.
Last of all, there is repetition in the *Beowulf* aside from the

---

[9] Numbers in the second column refer to the earlier accounts.

three main incidents of the poem. In ll. 2200-2210 we have mentioned the death of Higelac, the slaying of his successor, Heardred, by the Swedes, and the accession of Beowulf. Since we have here only a reference, we cannot regard the more elaborate account of the death of Higelac and the events which followed (2354-2400) as repetition. The speech of the messenger, however, covers the same ground as some of the above and repeats some of the facts of Beowulf's speech (2426-2509), such as the slaying of Hæthcyn (2923-2927) and the slaying of Ongentheow (2977-2990), which have already been brought out in ll. 2482-2483; 2484-2489.

We might also regard as repetition the second description of Heremod (1709-1722) as the type of a bad king. We should be a little unjust in doing so, however, as the two descriptions are not the same. In the first (901-913) we learn that Heremod was delivered into the hands of his foes, that he was a great burden to his people, and that his subjects were eager to have his son rule in his stead. The second description repeats that he was hated by his people, and adds that he slew his companions, that his spirit was murderous, that he gave no jewels, and that he was without joy.

The *Beowulf* has, then, about 280 lines, or 9 per cent. of the poem, given up to repetition, while the *Juliana* has only 0.6 per cent., the *Andreas* only 1 per cent., and the *Elene* only 1 per cent. Therefore, we conclude that from this point of view the *Juliana*, the *Elene*, and the *Andreas* show a marked advance upon the *Beowulf* in narrative style.

Of much greater importance is the study of repetition for the light which it throws upon ''inner history.'' The repetitions in the *Beowulf* are of three kinds. In the first case, there is the natural, summarizing repetition, when one of the characters of the story must be informed of something of which the reader is already cognizant. Of this kind are Beowulf's brief accounts of his adventures before Hrothgar (957-979; 1651-1670), Hrothgar's statements of his hopelessness (929-942), Wiglaf's account of the fight with the dragon (2873-2883) and his account of the last moments of Beowulf (3084-3100), and the messenger's account of the fight with the dragon (2900-2910). In all of these cases the repetitions follow the first accounts naturally. Of the same kind are the repetitions of the accounts of the Mermedonians in the *Andreas* (174-182; 279-282) and of the fate of Matthew among them (183-188). They are natural summaries where information is to be conveyed from one character in the story to another.

In the second case, there is in the *Beowulf* repetition which seems to be due to the fact that the author is unable to express all of the details present to his mind in one picture. We have this kind of repetition in the statement that Grendel is charmed against the sword (987-990), in the second account of the damage to Heorot (997-1002), in the summary of the dragon's life and death (2826-2845), and in the description of the dragon (3038-3046). These repetitions are of the same kind as the single one in the *Juliana,* the two in the *Elene,* and those of the *Christ,* where the second account follows close upon the first and adds to it new details.

The frequency of these repetitions of the first and the second kind in the *Beowulf* seems to indicate that the method of composition of that poem was in general looser than that of the *Juliana,* the *Elene,* and the *Andreas.* But this indication is not very positive, since these repetitions are all quite natural. We feel that they could have occurred in a later poem as well as in an earlier, in a Christian poem as well as in a pagan, in a poem handed down and modified by scops as well as in a poem written by one self-conscious individual.

Not so with the third kind of repetition, which we find in the *Beowulf* alone. In this case we have a repetition which is not the natural summary where it is necessary for the progress of the story for one character to inform another of what has taken place. Neither is it the second picture which immediately follows the first and supplements it with new details. It is an unnecessary repetition which might be accounted for by either one of two main theories,—first, that the events of the story became vague in the mind of the minstrel during the recital of the poem, that he did not grasp the story as a whole; or, second, that the writer of the *Beowulf* embodied in his poem a number of accounts which were once separate. Each of these views is improbable.

The first assumes that the story was written down just as it came from the mouth of the minstrel. The second assumes that the long poem is largely a compilation of varying, shorter poems.

But how, then, do we account for this repetition in the *Beowulf?* The earliest versions of the story were perhaps marked by repetition, exact verbal repetition. And repetition was popular with the poet and with his audience. With the development under epic treatment repetition tended to disappear.[10] In the *Beowulf* it still remains; not, however, as exact verbal repetition, but as conscious modification. The final poet of the *Beowulf,* I think, was familiar with the heroic epic which was marked by repetition. He retained this characteristic which had come down from the earliest pagan poems about Beowulf. He retained repetition as a traditional mark of the heroic epic. But he was too much of an artist to retain it as exact verbal reproduction or as repetition without additions of details. He consciously modified his different accounts of the same event for the sake of variety.

Thus, we see, although we regard the *Beowulf* as the product of a self-conscious poet of the time of Cynewulf, although we regard it as the product of a Christian who aimed primarily to emphasize the evil of the descendants of Cain, although we regard it as the product of a poet who aimed primarily to instruct a future king, yet we must grant that it has in repetition a development of one of the characteristics of the earlier pagan epic, that it represents a stage of development nearer to the pagan, heroic epic than is that represented by the Christian epics.

Of the relation of the Christian epics to the Latin we need mention here only that the natural Old English tendency to delay, to wander from the straightforward path, to lose sight of the perspective of the whole, was confirmed by the Latin prose legends of the saints and by the Latin Christian poems. The delays in the *Juliana,* the *Elene,* the *Andreas,* and the *Christ* are due to the influence of the older English poems like the *Beowulf* and to the confirming influence of the Latin.

---

[10] Gummere, *The Popular Ballad,* p. 124.

VII.

SUMMARY AND CONCLUSION.

Now, in conclusion, let us sum up the results of our study of the Christian epics,

A. Aside from their relation to the *Beowulf* and to the Latin literature accessible to the author or authors;

B. In relation to the Beowulf, and

C. In relation to the Latin.

A.—1.

We have found that the Old English Christian epics which we have been studying fall into two main divisions. In the one are the *Juliana*, the *Elene*, and the *Andreas*. In the other stands alone the *Christ*. We have found in the first place, that in the poems of the first division the fundamental conception is in each case Christianity versus paganism or Judaism, the combination of a single dominant thought, a single controlling passion, and a single mood of the mind. This fundamental conception involves the main interests of the Old English life of its time,— violent action, with pagan ideals of strength, loyalty, courage, revenge, generosity, wisdom, and acquiescence in the decrees of fate, and Christianity, with the new ideals of love, faith, and self-sacrifice. It is a high and universally human conception, developed through the conflict between Christianity and paganism or Judaism.

The fundamental conception of the *Christ*, the poem of the second division, is the coming of the Lord, a combination of a single mood of the mind and a single dominant thought. It, too, involves the main interests of the Old English life of its time. It is developed through a series of expressions of the emotions of the believer, through a series of pictures of the Advent and of the Day of Doom, and through a series of lessons drawn from the three-fold Advent. Here, again, the fundamental conception is high and universally human.

In both divisions the fundamental conceptions show the

typically Christian, hopeful treatment of a tragic theme. And in both divisions, in spite of the mixture of the old ideals with the new, there is no case of a central motif which is not Christian.

Second, we have seen that the general form employed to develop the fundamental conceptions of the poems of the first division is the rather long, narrative poem, the Christian epic, in language, meter, structure, and style similar to the heroic epic. And while the *Christ*, except in the second division, lacks to a great extent the element of narrative objectivity, perhaps the most essential quality of the epic, it, too, is similar to the heroic epic in language and meter, and it has many epic characteristics.

Third, we have found that the poems of the first division have the unity that lies in the single action with its beginning, its middle, and its end. This single action is developed in each case according to the common structural plan of the drama with a central climax. But in each case the admission of digressive or subordinate material tends to destroy the unity of the main action. The *Juliana* and the *Andreas* devote much space to digression. And the *Elene* includes, besides a rather long digression, a useless subordinate action.

The inclusion of this digressive material makes the emphasis of space in each case weak, least so in the *Elene*, most in the *Juliana*. But the emphasis of position is strong in the *Juliana* and in the *Andreas*. And it is strong within the main plot of the *Elene*, although this poem is weakened by the sub-plot at the end.

Then, the coherence of each of these poems is excellent in the general order of events. In the *Juliana* and in the *Andreas*, but not in the *Elene*, the coherence is good, too, in the logical sequence of events.

In the *Christ* we have found the unity to be that of mood. The poem is not concerned with one main action. Its unity lies in its appeal to the emotions. This is weakened by undue stress upon an appeal to the intellect, by the inclusion of an undue amount of exposition. Its unity is weakened, also, by abrupt changes in style or method and by the lack of a definite order or progress.

The emphasis in the *Christ* on each of the three main parts is good, both from the point of view of position and from that of space. But, within each of these parts the emphasis is weak, because too much space is given up to exposition.

And the coherence of the *Christ*, while it is good within the smaller divisions of the poem, is very weak in that there is only the loosest connection between the larger parts.

Fourth, we have seen that the plots of the poems of the first division, the *Juliana*, the *Elene*, and the *Andreas*, are developed by simple objective narrative, by subjective narrative, by description, by comment on the action or exposition, and by direct discourse. We should note, in particular, that the *Juliana* has little objective narrative, less subjective, practically no description, and no comment on the action; that the *Elene* has some description and much very specific narration and but little comment on the action; and that the *Andreas* has description for its own sake more positively than has the *Elene*, that it has a unique comment on the action in which the author regrets his inability to tell the life of Andrew adequately, and that it adds the methods of general narration and general description.

We should note specially that of all the methods of development by far the most important is direct discourse. In the *Juliana* dialogue is primarily the formal colloquy. There is no natural talk, although there are approaches to it; and there is only one case where we have more than two speakers. But in spite of their formality the colloquies tend to become dramatic, —they portray critical situations. Then, the *Juliana* contains both the dramatic monologue and the tedious, didactic monologue. In the *Elene*, too, dialogue is primarily the formal colloquy. There are only rare approaches to natural conversation. There is no case where we have more than two speakers. And the colloquies rarely portray dramatic situations. Here the typical form of direct discourse is the long, formal monologue. But in the *Andreas* dialogue is not always the formal colloquy. There is a much nearer approach to natural conversation; and in four places we have more than two speakers. Then, the dialogue is also more dramatic. Here the long, formal monologue has little place.

In these poems direct discourse which does not advance the action serves to impart general information, to impart information essential to the understanding of the story, to portray character, to give verisimilitude and variety, and to give authority to the statements of the author. Direct discourse is the main method of advancing the action in the *Juliana*. And in the *Elene* and in the *Andreas* it is a prominent factor at each important step in the movement of the plot.

Thus in each of these poems there is much variety, in the methods of development as well as in the actions and characters themselves.

The *Christ*, the poem of the second division, is also developed by simple objective narrative, by subjective narrative, by description, and by exposition or comment on the action. But in it much more space is given up to description and to exposition of a wide range; and in it are added the very important methods of lyric outbursts of praise, exhortation, and supplication.

In the *Christ*, too, direct discourse is very important. Of particular importance is the approach to realistic conversation in the dramatic colloquy of Joseph and Mary. Here the long, formal monologue is not found. In its place we have the long supplication and the quotation for authority.

The Christ also has direct discourse which does not advance the action and that which does. The first serves to impart information, to give verisimilitude and variety, to summarize actions preceding those of the main account, and to give authority. The second is rare because the poem has little action. But wherever the account becomes narrative, direct discourse has an important place in the action. Thus, the *Christ*, too, has much variety in methods of development as well as in subject matter.

Finally, we have seen that the plot movement in each of the poems of the first division is simple. There is no complication. In no case does the author handle synchronous actions.

Moreover, the plot movement in each case would be swift were it not for the delays common to Old English poetry. In the *Juliana* there are many actions in small space, but the story is delayed by a tedious discourse by the Devil. The *Elene* is delayed by comment on the action and by digression. Aside from this, while by no means slow, the story is not so swift as the *Juliana,* on account of a tendency to become didactic at important points of the action. The *Andreas* is delayed by comment, by digression, and by episode. Aside from this, the movement, while not so swift as that of the *Juliana,* is swifter than that of the *Elene.*

The poem of the second division, the *Christ,* has little movement. The lyric and didactic material of Part I has no progress. At the beginning of Part II we have a simple narrative movement without delay. Part III contains a series of supplementary pictures which move slowly over the events of the Day of Doom. The progressive movement is not marked, on account of the frequent backward movement in the repetition of the preceding picture. While there are no digressions and no episodes, the unprogressive lyrics, the brief comments of the author, the longer expository accounts, and the repetitions destroy all sense of movement.

Conclusion as to the comparative worth of
the poems

A.—2.

Now that we have summarized our study of the *Juliana,* the *Elene,* the *Andreas,* and the *Christ* as independent poems, we should ask first, whether that study has furnished material which is of value in determining the comparative worth of these poems, and, second, whether that study throws any light upon the vexed question of the authorship of the *Andreas.*

To the first question we may answer that we cannot judge the *Christ* in comparison with the others, for to do so would be to determine the relative value of epic and lyric. Then, we may add that the *Juliana* undoubtedly is of a lower order than the *Elene* or the *Andreas.* The tedious digression of the *Juliana,* proportionally much longer than the digressions of the other poems, and the lack of concreteness in the narrative style make this work dull. Yet we should note that, aside from the one, long digression, the *Juliana* is of much importance, first, because its action is restricted more positively than that of the *Elene* or that of the *Andreas* to a single series of events causally related; and, second, because it is developed almost exclusively by direct discourse.

But it is not so easy from the point of view of our study to determine the relative merits of the *Elene* and the *Andreas*. We can best arrive at a conclusion, perhaps, by noting the characteristic defects and the characteristic virtues of the two poems. Both are weak in that the movement of the events is delayed. In the *Andreas* the discourse on the sea (469-817) is proportionally twice as long as the digressive speech of Judas in the *Elene* (411-546); yet the first is in itself more interesting than the second and it is introduced in the portion of the *Andreas* where delay may best be tolerated, while the second immediately precedes the central climax of the *Elene*.

Then, the *Elene* is weakened by the subordinate plot which stands at the end, by the fact that there are three main protagonists, Constantine, Elene, and Judas, and by the rather didactic speeches of Elene and Judas at crucial points of the action. On the other hand, the *Andreas* is weakened by the lack of a sufficient human motif for Andrew's tortures. But, as we have noted, we must disregard this in a poem which is concerned with the supernatural. And the *Andreas* is weakened, but only in a minor way, by incompleteness in dropping Matthew and the followers of Andrew from the story, and by inconsistency in disregarding the bodies of the slain guards when the Mermedonian cannibals are starving.

Thus, it seems to me, the defects of the *Andreas* are less marked than those of the *Elene*. When we turn to the characteristic virtues, we find, first of all, that both poems have passages of vivid, specific narrative unsurpassed in the whole field of Old English poetry. But the *Elene* is surpassed by the *Andreas* in this respect, for while in the former that kind of narrative is limited to the introduction (18-143; 225-265), with a touch of it here and there in the rest of the poem, as in 1105-1116, in the latter it is much more common.[1]

Then, there is more variety in the *Andreas*. There is nothing in the *Elene* which is equal to the more natural, more varied, and more dramatic direct discourse of the *Andreas*. And finally, we should note that the defects of the *Andreas* are more pardonable and the virtues more worthy of praise, because the action of

[1] See ll. 40-58; 235-247; 369-381; 465-467; 836-843; 1219-1280; 1446-1449; 1522-1553.

this poem is more difficult to handle than is that of the *Elene*. In the *Elene* there is but one active force, except for the brief passage of conflict between Judas and the heroine. In the *Andreas* there is throughout the poem the action and reaction of two strong forces in conflict.

Thus, from the point of view of our study, we must rank the *Juliana* lowest in the scale of excellence, the *Elene* next, and the *Andreas* highest.

While we cannot judge the *Christ* in comparison with the other poems, we should note that in spite of the fact that it is loosely constructed, that it has abrupt changes of form, and that it is weakened by much didactic exposition, we must give it praise as an attempt at an elaborate art form probably unknown in English literature up to its time. And, moreover, although this attempt was not very successful, the author of the poem outshone his predecessors and his contemporaries in producing impassioned lyrics of a new order in English literature and sublime, imaginative pictures of the Day of Doom far beyond anything else in the English literature of their time.

Conclusion as to the authorship of the Andreas

A.—3.

In answer to the second question, whether our study throws any light upon the problem of the authorship of the *Andreas,* we must answer that it has served only to emphasize the fact that the problem is probably insoluble. If the author's name were not signed to any of the poems, we should say that the *Juliana* is the work of an inferior poet, that the *Elene* is the work of a greater poet, that the *Andreas* is the work of a poet still greater, and that the *Christ* is the work of a poet perhaps greater than the others but of a distinctly different type. The more vivid, concrete narrative style, the more varied, more realistic, and more dramatic direct discourse, and the colloquies between more than two persons in the *Andreas* point to an author greater than the author of the *Elene.* But since there is such marked progress from the *Juliana* to the *Elene,* Cynewulf's technique may very well, still later, have risen to the excellence of the *Andreas.* Since we know that the widely differing poems of the *Juliana,* the *Elene,* and the *Christ* are from the same hand; since we must consider the development of power in the same poet, writing at different times, under varying conditions, for different purposes; and since we must regard the more or less close following of sources, and must admit the possibility of a school of writers or of close imitation; we must conclude that while Cynewulf's authorship of the *Andreas* is probable, we can say no more.

The Juliana, the Elene, the Andreas and the Christ in comparison with the Beowulf

B.

When we come to summarize the results of our study of the Christian epics in comparison with the *Beowulf*, our first main conclusion is that the *Juliana*, the *Elene*, and the *Andreas* represent a stage of narrative development more advanced than that of the *Beowulf*, is so far as

1. They narrow their plots to single main actions, while the *Beowulf* contains more than one main action;

2. They include less digressive and episodic material;

3. They contain more of the note of personal emotion;

4. In them direct discourse is less formal and more dramatic, and it is employed to develop the action of the plot; and

5. The movement of their plots is swifter and more direct; and that the *Beowulf* in turn represents a stage of narrative development more advanced than that of the *Juliana*, the *Elene*, and the *Andreas*, only in so far as

1. It contains one clear instance of the treatment of synchronous actions, while the other poems have nothing of the kind; and

2. It contains more of the author's comment on the action of the story.

Now this apparent contradiction is explained by the second main conclusion from this part of our study, namely, that the *Beowulf* follows to a certain extent an older version of the story. The final poet of the *Beowulf* was perhaps as great a poet as Cynewulf. He is able to give a marked unity to the individual parts of his story; he employs with much skill most of the methods of plot development found in the Christian epics; he shows an advance in narrative development in his treatment of synchronous actions and in his personal comments. But in other respects his poem represents a lower stage of development because it follows the form of the older heroic epic, which was developed through the songs of scops.

This assumption is strengthened,

1. By the fact that the fundamental conception and the motivation of the *Beowulf* point back to an earlier heroic epic which was not Christian;

2. By the fact that in the *Beowulf* the inclusion of a number of main incidents, not strongly related, in general, represents a method of composition looser than that of the Christian epics;

3. By the fact that the formal, occasional speeches which do not advance the action suggest the tendency of the scop toward rhetorical effects in the recitation of his long, perhaps rambling story;

4. By the fact that much digression is characteristic of the method of the scop;

5. By the fact that much episode is characteristic of the method of the scop; and

6. By the fact that much of the repetition in the *Beowulf* can be accounted for only by the influence of the older poem of the scop.

The third main conclusion from this part of our study is that there is almost nothing in the Christian epics which we could not account for, if we desired to do so, without going outside of the field of Old English literature. The fundamental conceptions and the motivation of the *Juliana,* the *Elene,* the *Andreas,* and the *Christ* are the natural results of the influence of the older heroic epic combined with the influence of Christianity. The general form, metrical and structural, of the *Juliana,* the *Elene,* and the *Andreas* is the same as that of the *Beowulf.* The general metrical form of the *Christ* is also the same, and its general structural form might be accounted for by the teaching of the Church in regard to the three-fold celebration of the Advent. In more detail, the stricter unity of action in the Christian epics might be a natural development from the *Beowulf.* And so might be the less formal, more realistic direct discourse of the Christian epics. The increase of lyric and dramatic elements in the Christian epics, again, might be natural developments from the material of the *Beowulf* and other Old

English poems and from the general influence of Christianity. And the swifter movement of plot in the Christian epics would be a natural result of the narrowing of the field of incidents.

The Juliana, the Elene, the Andreas and the Christ in comparison with the Latin

C.

Finally, when we come to sum up the results of our study of the Christian epics in comparison with the Latin literature which was accessible to their author or authors, we find first that the Old English poems were practically uninfluenced by the Vergilian epics.

We find, however, that the Latin prose legends of the saints confirmed the author or authors of the *Juliana,* the *Elene,* and the *Andreas* in the natural tendency to unify the plots of these poems and in the characteristic Old English tendency to digress from the main line of action; and that the Latin hymns and dramatic colloquies of the early church confirmed the author or authors in the tendency to increase the lyric and dramatic elements in these poems.

And we find in case of the *Christ* that this new form in Old English literature might be accounted for as a natural development of what lies in the *Beowulf* and other Old English poems and as a natural result of the attitude of heart and mind occasioned by Christianity. We have noted that the general form of the trilogy, while it may have been influenced by certain Latin poems, is best accounted for by the attitude of the church toward the festival of the Advent and by Latin prose sermons expounding the same. And we have noted that the new lyric, dramatic, and emotionally expository elements of the *Christ,* all having their beginnings in other Old English poems, owe much to the Latin prose of the service, to the Latin dramatic colloquies, to the sermons, and to the hymns of the early church.

BIBLIOGRAPHY.

BIBLIOGRAPHY.[1]

ALCUIN: De Pontificibus et Sanctis Ecclesiae Eboracensis. (Migne, Patrologiae Cursus Completus, Series Latina Prior, v. 101.)

AUGUSTINE: Confessions. (Migne, v. 32).

AVITUS: De Mosaicae historiae gestis. (Migne, v. 59.)

BEDA: Historia Ecclesiastica Gentis Anglorum, ed. Stevenson. London, 1838.

CHADWICK, H. MUNRO: Beowulf and other Early National Poems. Cambridge History of English Literature, chap. III. New York, 1907.

COMPARETTI, DOMENICO: Vergil in the Middle Ages. Translated by E. F. M. Benecke. New York, 1895.

COOK, ALBERT S.: The Christ of Cynewulf. Boston, 1900.

EBERT, ADOLF: Allgemeine Geschichte der Literatur des Mittelalters im Abendlande bis zum Beginne des XI Jahrhunderts. I. Band., 2. Aufl. Leipzig, 1889.

EMERSON, O. F.: Legends of Cain. (Publ. Mod. Lang. Assoc., N. S., v. XIV.)

GARNETT, JAMES A.: The Latin and the Anglo-Saxon Juliana. (Publ. Mod. Lang. Assoc. N. S., vol. VII.)

GOLLANCZ, ISRAEL: Cynewulf's Christ. London, 1892.

GREEN, J. R.: A History of the English People. Book I. New York, 1878.

—— The Making of England. New York, 1882.

GUMMERE, FRANCIS B.: The Popular Ballad. Boston, 1907.

HART, WALTER M.: Ballad and Epic. (Harvard Studies and Notes in Philology and Litterature, v. XI, 1907.)

HVEMER, JOHANNES: Gai Vetti Aquilini Iuvenci Evangeliorum Libri Quattuor. (Corpus Scriptorum Ecclesiasticorum Latinorum, v. XXIV.)

JANSEN, KARL: Die Cynewulf-Forschung von ihren Anfängen bis zur Gegenwart. (Bonner Beiträge zur Anglistik, Heft XXIV.)

JEROME: Epistola XXII ad Eustochium. (Migne, Sancti Eusebii Hieronymi Opera Omnia, v. I, pp. 394-425.)

KENT, CHAS. W.: Elene, An Old English Poem, Edited with Introduction, Latin Original, Notes, and Complete Glossary. Boston, 1891.

KER, W. P.: Epic and Romance. New York, 1897.

---

[1] The list contains only those works which I have used in the preparation of this thesis. For more elaborate bibliographies see Strunk, *Juliana*, pp. 61-68; Kent, *Cynewulf's Elene*, pp. 14-17; Krapp, *Andreas and the Fates of the Apostles*, pp. lxxiii-lxxviii; Cook, *The Christ of Cynewulf*, Introduction and Notes; Jansen, *Bonner Beiträge zur Anglistik*, Heft xxiv.

—— The Dark Ages. New York, 1904.

KRAPP, GEORGE P.: Andreas and the Fates of the Apostles. Two Anglo-Saxon Narrative Poems, Edited with Introduction, Notes, and Glossary. Boston, 1906.

PANCOAST, HENRY S.: An Introduction to English Literature. New York, 1895.

SEDGEFIELD, WALTER J.: King Alfred's Old English Version of Boethius' De Consolatione Philosophiae. Oxford, 1899.

SEDULIUS: Hymnus II. Carmen Paschale. (Corpus Script. Eccles. Lat., v. X.)

SMITH, M. BENTINCK: Old English Christian Poetry. Chap. IV of Cambridge Hist. of Eng. Lit. New York, 1907.

STRUNK, WILLIAM: Juliana. Boston, 1904.

TAYLOR, HENRY O.: The Classical Heritage of the Middle Ages. New York, 1901.

WÜLKER, RICHARD PAUL: Bibliothek der Angelsächsischen Poesie. Begründet von Christian W. M. Grein. II. Band., 1. Hälfte. Kassel, 1888; II, 2, Leipzig, 1894; III, 1, Leipzig, 1897.

—— Geschichte der englischen Litteratur von den ältesten Zeiten bis zur Gegenwart. 2 Aufl. Leipzig, 1906.

—— Grundriss zur Geschichte der angelsächsischen Litteratur. Mit einer Übersicht der Angelsächsischen Sprachwissenschaft. Leipzig, 1885.

WYATT, A. J.: Beowulf. Cambridge, 1898.

INDEX

A

Acircius, 12
Adam, 63
Adrian, 11
Aeneas, 13
Aeneid, 18
Aeschere, 74, 92
Africanus, 59, 77
Aidan, 11
Alcuins, 12, 14
Aldhelm, 12
Ambrose, 12
Andreas, 13, 17, 18, 19, 21, 22, 24, 27, 31, 35, 36, 37, 38, 39, 40, 47, 48, 49, 50, 51, 53, 54, 55, 56, 57, 58, 59, 60, 65, 66, 67, 69, 70, 71, 79, 80, 81, 82, 84, 86, 88, 89, 90, 96, 97, 98, 99, 100, 101, 102, 103, 105, 106, 107, 109, 110, 111, 112, 115
Andrew, 17, 18, 19, 21, 22, 24, 27, 31, 32, 36, 38, 39, 40, 41, 56, 59, 60, 61, 65, 66, 67, 69, 79, 80, 81, 82, 90, 101, 106
Arator, 12
Athanasius, 12
Auctor, 12
Augustine, St., 11, 12, 13, 14
Avitus, Alcimus, 12

B

Baducing, Benedict 11
Basil, 12
Bede, 12, 13, 50
Beowulf, 11, 20, 21, 24, 25, 30, 47, 48, 50, 69, 70, 71, 72, 73, 74, 75, 79, 84, 85, 86, 87, 88, 89, 90, 91, 92, 93, 94, 95, 96, 97, 98, 99, 111, 112, 115
Bernard, St., 49
Biscop, Benedict, 11, 12
Boethius, 12

C

Caedmon, 12
Cain, 20, 93, 98
Carmen, 49
Cassiodorus, 12
Chaucer, 15
Christ, 13, 15, 17, 19, 20, 21, 22, 24, 29, 32, 33, 34, 35, 36, 37, 39, 40, 41, 42, 43, 44, 45, 46, 48, 49, 50, 51, 52, 54, 56, 57, 58, 59, 61, 63, 67, 68, 69, 70, 71, 78, 80, 81, 82, 83, 84, 86, 90, 91, 97, 98, 99, 100, 101, 102, 103, 105, 107, 109, 112, 115,
Chrysostom, 12
Cicero, 12
Clemens, 12
Comminianus, 12
Constantine, 28, 29, 30, 53, 65, 78, 106
Cook, 43
Corippus, 12
Cynewulf, 12, 15, 16, 21, 36, 39, 40, 44, 47, 49, 53, 86, 87, 98, 109, 110, 111

D

Daeghrefn, 88
Dante, 15
Devil, 17, 19, 20, 27, 28, 30, 31, 35, 36, 40, 48, 59, 62, 63, 64, 65, 66, 67, 68, 69, 71, 77, 78, 79, 80, 89, 102
Dido, 13
Donatus, 12

E

Elene, 13, 17, 18, 19, 21, 22, 24, 27, 28, 29, 30, 33, 35, 36, 37, 38, 39, 40, 47, 48, 49, 50, 51, 52, 53, 55, 56, 57, 58, 59, 60, 61, 63, 64, 65, 66, 67, 68,